MAN IN
THE MODERN AGE

AMS PRESS
NEW YORK

MAN IN
THE MODERN AGE

By

K. JASPERS

PROFESSOR IN THE UNIVERSITY OF HEIDELBERG

Translated by

EDEN *and* CEDAR PAUL

NEW YORK

HENRY HOLT AND COMPANY

1933

Library of Congress Cataloging in Publication Data

Jaspers, Karl, 1883-1969.
    Man in the modern age.

    Translation of Die geistige Situation der Zeit.
    Reprint of the 1933, ed. published by H. Holt, New York.
    1. Civilization, Modern—20th century. I. Title.
CB425.J342 1978   909.82   75-41155
ISBN 0-404-14558-2

From the edition of 1933, New York
First AMS edition published in 1978
Manufactured in the United States of America

AMS PRESS INC.
NEW YORK, N.Y.

CONTENTS

Contents

CONTENTS

MAN IN THE MODERN AGE

INTRODUCTION

For more than a century, the problem concerning the situation of mankind has been growing ever more urgent, and each generation has endeavoured to solve that problem according to its own lights. But whereas in former days only a few were anxiously considering the dangers to which our mental world is exposed, since the war the gravity of the peril has become manifest to every one.

The topic, however, is not merely inexhaustible, but insusceptible of fixed definition, inasmuch as it undergoes modification even while our attention is being concentrated on it. Past situations can be regarded as finished, as having had the curtain rung down on them, as having had their day and ceased to be; whereas the stimulating characteristic of a present situation is that thinking about it helps to determine its upshot.

Every one knows that the extant world-situation is not definitive.

There were periods in which man felt his world to be durable, an unchanging intermediate between the vanished Golden Age and the End that would come in due course when the Almighty's purposes were fulfilled. Man accommodated himself to life as he found it, without wishing to change it. His activities were limited to an endeavour to better his own position amid environing circumstances deemed to be substantially unalterable. Within these circumstances he had safe harbourage, linked as he was both with heaven and with earth. The world was his own world, even though it was of no account, because for him true being existed only in a transcendental realm.

As compared with man in those eras, man to-day has been uprooted, having become aware that he exists in what is but a historically determined and changing situation. It is as if the foundations of being had been shattered. How self-evident to the man of old seemed the unity of life and knowledge has become plain to us now that we realise that the life of our fellows in the past was spent under conditions in which reality was, as it were, veiled. We, on the other hand, have become able to see things as they really are, and that is why the foundations of life quake beneath our feet; for, now that the identity of thought and being (hitherto unchallenged) has ceased to exist for us, we see only, on the one hand, life, and, on the other, our own and our companions' awareness of that life. We do not, as did our forefathers, think merely of the world. We ponder how it is to be comprehended, doubting the validity of every interpretation; and behind every apparent unity of life and the consciousness of life there looms the distinction between the real world and the world as we know it. That is why we live in a movement, a flux, a process, in virtue of which changing knowledge enforces a change in life; and, in turn, changing life enforces a change in the consciousness of the knower. This movement, this flux, this process, sweeps us into the whirlpool of unceasing conquest and creation, of loss and gain, in which we painfully circle, subject in the

main to the power of the current, but able now and
then to exert ourselves within a restricted sphere of
influence. For we do not only live in a situation
proper to mankind at large, but we experience this
situation as it presents itself in specific historical
circumstances, issuing out of a previous situation and
progressing towards a subsequent one.

The result is that our consciousness of the movement, in which we ourselves are one of the factors,
has a strange twofoldedness. Since the world as we
now know it is not definitive, our hopes, no longer
anchored in the realm of the transcendental, have
turned towards the sublunary sphere, alterable by our
own endeavours, so that we have faith in the possibility of earthly perfectionment. On the other hand,
since (even in favourable situations) the individual
has no more than restricted powers of intervention,
and cannot fail to recognise that the actual results of
his doings depend far more upon general environing
conditions than upon the aims he is trying to fulfil;
since, therefore, he is made poignantly cognisant of
the small extent of his sphere of influence as compared with the vast possibilities of which he is abstractly
aware; and since, finally, the course of the world (which
no one is satisfied with) seems to him in many ways
undesirable—a feeling of powerlessness has become
rife, and man tends to regard himself as dragged along
in the wake of events which, when in a more sanguine
mood, he had hoped to guide. One inspired with a
religious conviction that man was as naught in face
of the transcendental was unperturbed by changing
events. Changes were the outcome of God's will,
and were not felt to clash with other conceivable
possibilities. To-day, however, the pride which aims
at universal understanding, and the arrogance of one

who regards himself as master of the world and therefore wants to mould it to his liking, knock at all doors, while their frustration arouses a feeling of terrible impotence. How man is to accommodate himself to this and rise superior to it, is one of the most vital questions of the present situation.

Man not only exists, but knows that he exists. In full awareness he studies his world and changes it to suit his purposes. He has learned how to interfere with "natural causation", insofar as this is merely the unconscious repetition of immutable similars. He is not merely cognisable as extant, but himself freely decides what shall exist. Man is mind, and the situation of man as man is a mental situation.

One who wishes to throw light on the present situation must begin by inquiring how it has hitherto been regarded, how it came into being, what in general a situation is, what aspects it displays, how the question as to the nature of man is to-day answered, and towards what future mankind is moving. The more clearly these questions are answered, the more decisively shall we pass through knowledge into the suspense of ignorance, and the quicker shall we reach the boundaries at which man in his isolation has become self-conscious.

1. Origin of the Epochal Consciousness

Man's critique of the times in which he lives is as old as man's self-consciousness. Our own critique of the contemporary era is rooted in the Christian conception of a historical process that moves towards the fulfilment of a plan of salvation. We have (for the most part) abandoned that conception, but our attitude to our epoch has either grown out of it or else has arisen in opposition to it. In the fulness of time appeared the Saviour, the Redeemer, and this marked the close of history; thenceforward our race had merely to await and to prepare for the Day of Judgment; the temporal world, whose end was close at hand, had become a nullity. As contrasted with the ideas set up against this, with the idea of a circulation of events, with that of a progressive culture, with that of the kingdom of this world, the Christian ideal, thanks to its universality, its uniqueness, its irrevocableness amid the history conceived in its womb, and its relation to the Person of the Redeemer, had an incomparable grip upon the individual. Although for the Christians the epoch in which they lived was the whole world, their awareness of that epoch as decisive in its character was enormously intensified.

This conception of history was transcendental. Historical events, insofar as they had already taken place, were the inscrutable consequences of the Fall, of the Mosaic revelation, of the mission of the Jews as the Chosen People, of the fulfilment of prophecy; or, insofar as they had still to come, were related only to the approaching end of the world. This world in its immanence had become substantially unhistorical, for it was deemed valueless. But when this transcendental outlook was changed into or replaced by one in which (though the sense of the uniqueness of the history of mankind was retained) the world was regarded as a movement, as an immanent progression, there awakened a consciousness in men's minds that their own epoch was somehow different from all that had preceded it, and they were at length animated by the feeling that—perhaps spontaneously and imperceptibly, perhaps through purposive effort on their part—something distinctive would grow out of it.

In the sixteenth century was severed the continuity

of the chain thanks to which, as generation followed generation, link after link passed on the consciousness of the epoch from one generation to another. The severance began with the deliberate secularisation of human life. The revival of classical learning, in conjunction with new schemes and new achievements in the domains of art, science, and technique, were effected by a coterie whose influence was Europe-wide. The mood of these innovators finds expression in the words of Ulrich von Hutten: "Minds are awakening, and it is a joy to be alive." It was an age of discovery. The world became known in all its seas and lands; the new astronomy was born; modern science began; the great era of technique was dawning; the State administrations were being nationalised. The idea of progress was conceived, and reached its climax during the eighteenth century. Whereas hitherto when men had looked forward it had been towards the end of the world and the Judgment Day, they now contemplated the perfectionment of civilisation. Rousseau determined to prick this bubble of self-satisfaction. In 1749, when a prize was offered for the best essay on the contribution of the arts and sciences to the improvement of public morals, he rejoined that they had corrupted morals, and he thus initiated the criticism which has ever since dogged the heels of the champions of progress.

The epochal consciousness entered a new phase. Beginning as a surge of mental activity which had not, in truth, recognised itself clearly as epochal, it was directed, first of all, towards the glamour of a well-ordered political life, and then towards human existence as such. Now were laid the foundations of the thought that, whereas hitherto life had been accepted as it was, the human reason was competent to mould life purposively, until it should become what it ought to be. The French Revolution was unprecedented in human history. Regarded as the opening of a new era wherein, guided by rational principles, man would shape his own destiny, it was at first enthusiastically acclaimed by the leaders of European thought.

In none of the earlier revolutions had there been any deliberate intention of transforming human society. Descartes, for instance, was not in revolt against the laws and conventions of his country, but ventured only to think of a revolution in the inner man. It was nonsensical, he declared, to propose the reform of a State by razing it to the ground and starting to rebuild it on entirely new foundations. Even the English revolution of the seventeenth century [German writers give this name to what British historians term the Great Rebellion, and not to the constitutional revolution of 1688] was rooted in religion and in the sense of national greatness. Protestantism, doubtless, renovated Christianity by a return to its fundamentals, but there was no attempt at secularisation. On the contrary, the gravamen of the Reformers' charge was that the Church had become a mundane institution. It was by their zeal for the reformed faith that Cromwell's Ironsides, who served God through the person of their chief, were inspired in the heroic struggle to advance the English (the chosen of God) to a position which would glorify Him and justify His choice. The French Revolution was the first revolution whose motive force was a determination to reconstruct life upon rational principles after all that reason perceived to be the weeds of human society had been ruthlessly plucked up and cast into the flames. Venerable tradition was to give no sanction! The only fore-runners of the French revolutionists had been the

Puritan refugees from England who had tried across the Atlantic to establish what they had failed to establish in their homeland; and these stalwarts, in days when secularisation was advancing, had gone so far as to proclaim the doctrine of the Rights of Man.

The surprising result of the French Revolution was that it underwent a transformation into its opposite. The resolve to set men free developed into the Terror which destroyed liberty. The reaction gathered strength; and hostility to the revolution, a fixed intention to prevent its recurrence, became the leading principle of all the States of Europe. Nevertheless, once revolution had occurred, men had become uneasy about the foundations of an existence for which they thenceforward held themselves responsible, since it could be purposively modified, and remoulded nearer to the heart's desire. Kant's prophecy of 1798 has remained true down to our own day: "Such a phenomenon in history can never be forgotten, inasmuch as it has disclosed in human nature the rudiment of and the capacity for better things which, prior to this, no student of political science had deduced from the previous course of events."

In actual fact, since the French Revolution there has prevailed a specifically new awareness of the epochal significance of the times. But in the nineteenth century this awareness was dichotomised, splitting, on the one hand, into faith in the coming of a splendid future, and, on the other, into horror of an abyss from which no rescue would be possible; but the hopes of some were dulled, and the fears of others were mitigated, when they came to regard their era as one of transition, this outlook having ever since been enough to calm and content the feeble in spirit.

At the outset of the period we are considering, the

philosophy of Hegel fashioned a peculiar epochal consciousness, giving expression to an unprecedented wealth of historical content in the extraordinarily supple and forcibly expressive dialectic method, which was charged with the affect of a conviction that the present had a unique significance. Dialectic disclosed the transformation of human consciousness by its own self. Each pulse of awareness was set in motion by self-awareness; every item of knowledge altered the knower; being thus altered, he must seek in his world a new knowledge of himself; in this way the stream flowed on unrestingly, for being and consciousness of being were severed, and they must perpetually renew their severance in a changed form, passing from one to the other; such was and is man's historical process. The how of the process was demonstrated by Hegel with a fulness and depth which have never been excelled. The unrest of man's self-consciousness was revealed in this thought of Hegel's, even though metaphysically hidden away in the totality of the spirit wherein all temporal particulars are subsumed; for in that totality of the spirit the temporal frenzy of human historical knowledge becomes the perfect repose of eternity.

The dialectic of the extant being and consciousness (which cannot be properly understood on a purely intellectual plane, but can only be adequately grasped in the momentous fulfilment of that within us which, through its claim to selfhood, provides the spirit with its capacity for greatness) was degraded by the fixed attachment of being to an artificially simplified process of human history—to history conceived as exclusively determined by the material conditions of production. I refer, of course, to Marxism. In this doctrine, dialectic sank to become nothing more than a method, devoid both of the content of historical human existence and of metaphysic. Thus, indeed, it rendered possible the formulation of problems whose study furnished an impetus to fruitful researches in connexion with certain specific historical and sociological problems. But at the same time it gave currency to catchwords falsely denominated scientific, these being the form wherein the profound historical epochal consciousness as originally conceived became base coin passing freely from hand to hand. At length even dialectic was jettisoned. There rose up against Marxism the economico-materialistic simplifications, and the naturalisations of human existence to species engaged in a blind mutual struggle. In these variants a genuine historical epochal consciousness had disappeared.

In the Hegelian dialectic an image of universal history was the mode in which the present became aware of itself; but there was an alternative possibility, that of ignoring the remote riches of concrete history, and of concentrating attention on the present. Fichte already developed such a critique in his *Grundzüge des gegenwärtigen Zeitalters*: and though his method was that of the abstract construction of a universal history from its beginning to its end (as the secularisation of the Christian philosophy of history), he kept his gaze fixed upon the kernel of Christian philosophy, wherein the present is regarded as the era in which sin has worked itself out to its conclusion. Kierkegaard was the first to undertake a comprehensive critique of his time, one distinguished from all previous attempts by its earnestness. This critique of his was the first to be applicable to the age in which we are now living, and reads as if it had been written but yesterday. He confronted man with nullity. Nietzsche, who wrote a few decades later, was unacquainted with the work of his predecessor Kierkegaard. He noted the advent of European nihilism, diagnosing its symptoms pitilessly. To their contemporaries these two philosophers seemed no more than freaks —prophets of a sensationalism which no one could take seriously. They were, in truth, pioneers who discerned what already existed but had not as yet aroused general disquiet, and only in our own day have they been acclaimed as thinkers dealing with contemporary actualities.

All through the nineteenth century the epochal consciousness, in comparison with that of Kierkegaard and Nietzsche, was obscure, but in many it was awaking. The public at large was content with culture and progress, but men of independent mind were full of uneasy forebodings. Goethe, for instance, wrote: "Mankind will become cleverer and more perspicacious, but not better nor happier nor more energetic. I foresee the day when God will no longer take delight in his creatures, and will once again have to annihilate the world and make a fresh start." In 1830 Niehbuhr, alarmed by the July revolution, penned the following jeremiad: "Unless God gives miraculous aid, we are faced by imminent destruction, akin to that which befell the Roman Empire towards the middle of the third century of the Christian era, when prosperity, freedom, culture, and science came to an end." Talleyrand said that those only who lived before 1789 could have tasted life in all its sweetness, and yet we of more than a century later look back to the opening period of the nineteenth century as a succession of halcyon days. Thus does each new generation shudder at the prospect of ruin while regarding as a Golden Age some earlier period in which those who belonged to it were harassed by the same gloomy vaticinations. In 1835 Tocqueville recognised the coming of democracy to be inevitable, and therefore, in his study of its nature, he was concerned, not with the thought of how to obviate it, but with that of how to minimise its evils. He and many others contemplated it as a sort of barbarian invasion. Burckhardt regarded its onset with horror. Earlier than this, in 1829, Stendhal, looking at the matter with cool objectivity, had written:

> In my opinion within a century liberty will kill the artistic sense. That sense is non-moral, since it misleads us into the ecstasy of love, into sloth and exaggeration. Put a man who has an artistic temperament in charge of the cutting of a canal, and instead of doing the work with the cold reasonableness proper to an engineer he will botch the job in one way or another.

Again:

> The bicameral system will go the round of the world, giving the death-blow to the fine arts. Instead of building a lovely church, rulers will make it their chief concern to invest their funds in America, so that, in the event of a change of government, they will be able to live there at ease. As soon as the two Houses rule I foresee, first of all, that they will never disburse twenty millions for fifty years in succession in order to build such an edifice as St. Peter's; and, secondly, that under their regime the drawing-rooms will be packed with wealthy persons who, though doubtless estimable, will not have had an education likely to cultivate their taste for the fine arts.

He advises artists who want to get on in the world to abandon art for sugar-planting or the manufacture of earthenware, for then they will "be more likely to become millionaires and members of parliament". In Ranke's diary for 1840 we read:

In former times great convictions were the rule, as the foundation of great endeavours. Nowadays people are satisfied to issue pronunciamentos. Nothing bears fruit; everything proves abortive. Those only achieve something who express the views of a political party and thence derive effective support.

To Cavour, the statesman, the coming of democracy seemed as inevitable as it did to Tocqueville, the investigator. Let me quote from Paléologue's *Cavour* parts of a letter written by the Italian statesman in 1835:

We can do nothing to avert it. Society is marching towards democracy with giant strides. . . . The nobility is decaying. . . . In the organisation of contemporary society there is no longer place for a patriciate. What means of defence have we against the inundation of the masses? Nothing stable, nothing effective, nothing durable. Is this a matter for congratulation or repining? I cannot say. Be it one or the other, it is, to my way of thinking, the inescapable future of mankind. Let us make ready for it then, or at least prepare our children for what is coming. . . . Modern society embodies a predestined evolution towards democracy, and any attempt to hinder the course of events would only induce storms without helping us to steer the ship into a safe anchorage.

Thus those who contemplated the future of mankind from the most multifarious outlooks were all, during the last century, inspired with a sense of danger. Man felt that his future was imperilled. Just as the Christian, convinced that this world was a lost world, had clung to his doctrine of salvation in which the world was transcended, so many of those to whom their epoch seemed a doomed epoch sought refuge in a contemplative assurance concerning essentials. Hegel, convinced that the age was one of decay, held that reality itself (and not philosophy alone) needed an atonement. Philosophy as the atonement of man was, he said, no more than a partial or external generalisation:

> In this connexion, philosophy is a separate sanctum, and its ministers constitute an isolated priesthood which must hold aloof from the world and whose function it is to safeguard the possession of truth. . . . Immediately practical matters are not the concern of philosophy.

Schiller wrote:

> In the bodily sense we want to be citizens of our own time (for, indeed, in that matter we have no choice); but in the mental sense it is the privilege and the duty of the philosopher and the imaginative writer to escape from the trammels of a particular nation and a specific time, becoming in the true sense of the word contemporaries of all ages.

Others have tried to lead their fellow-men back to Christianity. Take Grundtvig, for instance:

> Our generation stands at a parting of the ways, perhaps the most momentous known to history. The old has vanished and the new is still nebulous. No one can solve the riddle of the future. Where, then, can we discover peace of mind except in the Word which will stand fast when all the host of heaven is dissolved and when the heavens are rolled together as a scroll?

But Kierkegaard's position contrasts with these. He desires Christianity in its original purity, for this alone can help such a time as ours. Christianity must be resuscitated as the martyrdom of the individual, who is to-day annihilated by the mass-man. Kierkegaard will not allow himself to be vitiated by the prosperity of a secure position as pastor or professor; will not promulgate an objective theology or philosophy; will not become an agitator or a practical reformer. He cannot show his contemporaries what they ought to do, but can make them feel that they are on the wrong road.

These selections from the printed records of the epochal consciousness during the first half of the nineteenth century could be indefinitely multiplied, to show that nearly all the motifs of latter-day criticism are at least a century old. Before and during the Great War were penned the two most outstanding mirrors of our time: Rathenau's *Zur Kritik der Zeit* (1912) and Spengler's *Untergang des Abendlandes* (1918). Rathenau's book is a searching analysis of the mechanisation of modern life; Spengler's work is a philosophy of history, furnished with a wealth of observations, and attempting to demonstrate that the decay of the western world is the outcome of the operation of natural laws. The novel features of these two books are their material actuality, the way in which the ideas they put forward are sustained by positive data, the wide circulation they have achieved, and the increasing emphasis of their insistence that mankind stands face to face with annihilation. Still, Kierkegaard and Nietzsche remain the leaders in this field—though Kierkegaard has found no disciples to sustain his advocacy of primitive Christianity, and Nietzsche's Zarathustra philosophy has not been generally adopted. Since, however, both of them were revealers of the trend towards annihilation, it was only to be expected that the war should draw unprecedented attention to their doctrines.

Beyond question there is a widespread conviction that human activities are unavailing; that our learning is of dubious worth; that existence is no more than an unceasing maelstrom of reciprocal deception and self-deception by ideologies. Thus the epochal consciousness becomes detached from being, and is concerned only with itself. One who holds such a view cannot but be inspired with a consciousness of his own nullity. His awareness of the end as annihilation is simultaneously the awareness that his own existence is null. The epochal consciousness has turned a somersault in the void.

2. ORIGIN OF THE PRESENT SITUATION

More urgent than ever has become the problem concerning the present situation of mankind as the upshot of past developments and in view of the possibilities of the future. On the one hand we see possibilities of decay and destruction, and on the other hand we see possibilities that a truly human life is now about to begin; but as between these conflicting alternatives, the prospect is obscure.

The achievements that transformed the pre-human being into man were effected, not only before the days of recorded history, but even before tradition began. What lifted our forefathers above the animal world was the persistent and not merely fortuitous use of tools, the making and utilisation of fire, the birth of language, and a control of sexual jealousy sufficient to render possible comradeship and the foundation of durable societies. Recorded history, extending back for only six thousand years, is but a brief span in comparison with the hundreds of thousands of years of inaccessible pre-history during which these decisive steps in the making of man were being taken. In those long ages, men existed in various forms, widespread over the surface of the globe, knowing naught of one another. From among them western man (who has conquered the world, brought men of all parts into contact with one another, and made them aware of their common humanity) would seem to have developed in virtue of the consistent application of three great principles.

The first is rationalism, grounded upon Hellenic science, weighing and measuring the data of experience, and achieving their technical mastery. Universally valid scientific research, predictability of legal decisions thanks to the systematisation of Roman law, calculation applied to economic enterprise and pushed to the extent of rationalising all activity (even such as is arrested through being rationalised). These were the outcome of complete submission to the dominion of logical thought and empirical actuality as they disclose themselves to all persons and at all times.

The second principle is the subjectivity of selfhood which became explicit in the teachings of the Jewish prophets, in the wisdom of the Greek philosophers, and in the activities of the statesmen of classical Rome. What we term individuality developed along these lines in the men of the western world and was from the outset correlated with rationalism.

Coming to the third principle, we find in western man a firm conviction that the world is a tangible reality in space and time, this conviction being contraposed to the "unworldliness" of the East, which is the outcome of a sentiment that not-being is perhaps the essential reality of what presents itself to us as being. Assurance is assurance of this tangible reality and cannot arise independently thereof. Selfhood and rationalism are the twin sources of assurance, which cognises reality and seeks to master it.

Only during recent centuries have these three principles been developed, and not until the nineteenth century did they enter into their own. The surface of the world became universally accessible; space capitulated. For the first time man was enabled to dwell wherever he would on our planet. All things are interrelated. The technical mastery of space, time, and matter advances irresistibly, and no longer through casual and isolated discoveries, but thanks to organised collaboration, because of which discovery has been systematised and subjected to purposive endeavour.

After thousands of years during which civilisation progressed along detached and even divergent roads, the last four and a half centuries have witnessed the European conquest of the world, which the last hundred years have completed. During the acceleration of this concluding phase there was an abundance of independent and outstanding personalities; of persons animated by the pride of leadership, the delight of the master-craftsman, the fervour of the discoverer, venturesomeness tempered with discretion, the contentment of those who reach uttermost bourns: and there arose a sense of close kinship with the world thus revealed. To-day, however, we feel that for us this century of expansion is over and done with. There has been a reversal of mood, owing to which, though the positive achievements remain, we have come to recognise the persistence of vast and wellnigh insuperable difficulties. The movement of objective conquest seems to have attained its term; we no longer advance, but are inclined rather to retreat.

The guiding principles of western mankind are incompatible with the notion that a mere circular recurrence can be stable. Our reason tells us that every new cognition implies further possibilities. Reality does not exist as such, but has to be grasped by a cognition which is an active seizure. From century to century the rapidity of the relevant movements has increased. No longer is anything fixed. All things are put to the question and subjected to the requisite transformations; and of late this has been effected at the cost of internal frictions which were unknown in the nineteenth century.

The feeling of a breakaway from previous history is widespread. The innovation, however, is something more than a mere revolutionising of society in the sense of shattering it to bits, a change in property relationships, the overthrow of aristocracy. An ancient Egyptian papyrus dating from more than four thousand years ago contains the following passages:

> Robbers abound. . . . No one ploughs the land. People are saying: "We do not know what will happen from day to day." . . . Dirt prevails everywhere, and no longer does any one wear clean raiment. . . . The country is spinning round and round like a potter's wheel. . . . Slave-women are wearing necklaces of gold and lapis lazuli. . . . No more do we hear any one laugh. . . . Great men and small agree in saying: "Would that I had never been born." . . . Well-to-do persons are set to turn millstones. . . . Ladies have to demean themselves to the tasks of serving-women. . . . People are so famished that they snatch what falls from the mouths of swine. . . . The offices where records are kept have been broken into and plundered . . . and the documents of the scribes have been destroyed. . . . Moreover, certain foolish persons have bereft the country of the monarchy; . . . the officials have been driven hither and thither; . . . no public office stands open where it should, and the masses are like timid sheep without a shepherd. . . . Artists have ceased to ply their art. . . . The few slay the many. . . . One who yesterday was indigent is now wealthy, and the some-time rich overwhelm him with adulation. . . . Impudence is rife. . . . Oh that man could cease to be, that women should no longer conceive and give birth. Then, at length, the world would find peace.[1]

[1] Selections from Erman, *Die Literatur der Aegypten*, 1923, pp. 130–48.

We see from the foregoing that the feeling that social conditions are hopelessly disordered, and that no firm abiding-place remains, is not new to history. Thucydides' account of conditions in Hellas during the Peloponnesian war is another testimony from the ancient world.

But to strike home in the new times the notion must be more penetrating than can be a general conception of the possibilities of revolution, disorder, a loosening of moral ties. Since the days of Schiller, the modern mind has become aware of the loss of the sense of a divine presence in the world—a loss characteristic of recent centuries. In the West this process has been carried to a far greater extreme than elsewhere. Doubtless there were sceptics in ancient India and in the classical world, men for whom nothing but the immediate present, as it discloses itself to our senses, counted for anything—the immediate present, inexorably grasped, and itself accounted as null. But, even so, for them the world as a whole was still a spiritualised entity. In the West, as a sequel of the spread of Christianity, scepticism of another kind became possible. The idea of a transcendental creator, existing before, after, and apart from the world he had fashioned out of chaos, reduced that world to the level of a mere creature. The demons known to paganism vanished from the realm of nature, and the world became a godless world. All that had been created was now the object of human cognition, re-thinking (as it were) God's thoughts. Protestant Christianity took the matter very seriously. The natural sciences, with their rationalisation, mathematicisation, and mechanisation of the world, were closely akin to this form of Christianity. The great scientific investigators of the seventeenth and eighteenth centuries were pious Christians. But when, finally, advancing doubt made an end of God the Creator, there was left in being no more than the mechanical world-system recognised by the natural sciences—a world-system which would never have been so crudely denuded of spirit but for its previous degradation to the status of a creature.

The despiritualisation of the world is not the outcome of the unfaith of individuals, but is one of the possible consequences of a mental development which here has actually led to nothingness. We feel the unprecedented vacancy of existence, a sense of vacancy against which even the keenest scepticism of classical times was safeguarded by the richly-peopled fulness of an undecayed mythical reality, with which the *De rerum natura* of Lucretius the Epicurean is instinct. Such a development is not, indeed, absolutely inevitable to the human consciousness, for it presupposes a misunderstanding of the true significance of natural science and an unduly rigid application of its categories to all being. But, as aforesaid, it is possible; and it has actually occurred, having been promoted by the overwhelming successes of science in the technical and practical fields. What, in all the millenniums of human history and pre-history, no god had been able to do for man, man has done for himself. It is natural enough that in these achievements of his he should discern the true inwardness of being—until he shrinks back in alarm from the void he has made for himself.

Moderns are inclined to compare the present situation with that which prevailed during the decline of the classical systems, with the fall of the Greek States and the decay of Hellenism, or with the third century of the Christian era when ancient culture was collapsing.

Yet there are important differences. Classical civilisation was the civilisation of no more than a small part of the world, in an area which did not comprise within its bounds all the factors of the future of mankind. To-day, when communications are world-wide, the whole human race must enter the domain of western civilisation. At the beginning of the Dark Ages, population was declining; now it has increased and is still increasing beyond measure. Then the menace to civilisation came from without, now it comes from within. But the most conspicuous difference between our own time and the third century A.D. is that then technique was stationary or retrograde, whereas now it is advancing with giant strides. The favourable and unfavourable chances lie outside the range of possible prediction.

The objectively conspicuous new factor which cannot fail henceforward to modify the foundations of human existence, and thus provide it with new conditions, is this development of the world of technique. For the first time an effective control of nature has begun. If we think of our world as being buried, subsequent excavators would not bring to light any such beautiful objects as those which have come down to us from classical days, whose street-pavement, even, is a delight to us. They would, however, discover such vast quantities of iron and concrete as to make it plain that during the last few decades (as contrasted with all previous ages) man had begun to enwrap the planet in a mesh of apparatus. The step thus taken has been as momentous as that taken when our forefathers first began to use tools; and we can already look forward to the day when the world will become one vast factory for the utilisation of its matter and energy. For the second time man has broken away from nature to do work which nature would never have done for herself, and which rivals nature in creative power. This work becomes actualised for us, not only in its visible and tangible products, but also in its functioning; and our hypothetical excavator would not be able, from the vestiges of wireless masts and antennae, for instance, to infer the universality of the diffusion of news over the earth's surface.

The novelty of our century, the changes whose completion will set it so utterly apart from the past, are not, however, exhaustively comprised within the limits of the despiritualisation of the world and its subjection to a regime of advanced technique. Even those who lack clear knowledge of the subject are becoming decisively aware that they are living in an epoch when the world is undergoing a change so vast as to be hardly comparable to any of the great changes of past millenniums. The mental situation of our day is pregnant with immense dangers and immense possibilities; and it is one which, if we are inadequate to the tasks which await us, will herald the failure of mankind.

Is it an end that draws near, or a beginning? Is it perhaps a beginning as significant as that when man first became man, but now enriched by newly acquired means, and the capacity for experience upon a new and higher level?

3. SITUATION IN GENERAL

Hitherto when I have referred to a "situation", I have used the term abstractly and vaguely. Strictly speaking, only an individual can be said to be in a situation. By extension, we think of the situation of groups, States, mankind; of that of such institutions as the Church, the university, the theatre; of that of science, philosophy, art, literature. When the will of the individual espouses the cause of one of these things or institutions, his will and the cause he has espoused are in a situation.

In some instances, situations are unconscious, and become effective without awareness on the part of the person concerned. In other instances, situations are concretely regarded from the outlook of the self-conscious will of one who can accept them, utilise them, and transform them. A situation of which the observer or participator is conscious demands purposive behaviour in relation thereto. Its upshot is neither automatic nor inevitable, for it connotes possibilities within a certain range. What happens as a result of it is partly determined by the person who is in the situation, and by what he thinks about it. The "grasping" of a situation modifies it, insofar as the grasping of it renders possible the adoption of a definite attitude towards it and an appeal to the tribunal of action. To grasp a situation is the first step in the direction of its mastery; since to scrutinise it and to understand it arouse the will to modify its being. When I am still striving to understand the mental situation of the epoch, I am aspiring to exercise my faculties as a human being endowed with intelligence; and as long as my understanding remains incomplete, I can only think of the situation as working itself out independently of my contribution; but as soon as I become an active participator in the situation, I want reflectively to interfere with the action and reaction between the situation and my own existence.

We have to ask, however, what sort of situation I mean.

Man's being consists primarily of his existence in economic, sociological, and political situations, upon whose reality everything else depends, even though his being is not realisable simply through them alone.

Secondly, man's life as a conscious being lies within the realm of the cognisable. Historically acquired and now extant knowledge (regarded as to its content, its mode of acquisition, and its methodical classification and increase) is situation as the possible lucidity of man's mind.

Thirdly, what a man can himself become is, *qua* situation, determined by the other persons whom he encounters on his journey through life and by the possibilities of belief which appeal to him.

Thus when I am in search of the mental situation I must take into account actual being, the possible lucidity of knowledge, and the potentialities of belief.

(*a*) As regards his sociological existence, the individual is restricted to a specific environment, and is therefore not to an equal degree a participator in all environments. As yet the elements of a knowledge how man comports himself in all the extant sociological situations, is not available. Indeed, it is probable that few others know much about what, for the individual concerned, seems a matter of course in his daily experience.

To-day, doubtless, the individual has more mobility of status than ever before. Already in the nineteenth century a proletarian might rise to become a "captain of industry"; now he can become a minister of State and even a premier or the president of a republic. But, after all, such possibilities are open only to very few; and they are once more on the wane as compared with a man's enforced and uniform restriction to the lot into which he has been born.

People have acquired a certain amount of general knowledge regarding the main types of existence, such as that of the wage-earner, the salaried employee, the peasant, the handicraftsman, the entrepreneur, the civil servant. But the general fellowship of our human situation has been rendered even more dubious than before, inasmuch as, though the old ties of caste have been loosened, a new restriction of the individual to some prescribed status in the sociological machinery has become manifest. Less than ever, perhaps, is it possible for a man to transcend the limitations imposed by his social origins. What is to-day common to us all is not our humanity as a universal and all-pervading spirit of fellowship, but the cosmopolitanism of catchwords in conjunction with the spread of world-wide means of communication and the universalisation of certain pastimes. The general sociological situation is not the decisive factor in our destinies, being, rather, that which threatens us with annihilation. The decisive factor is the developing possibility of a selfhood which is not yet objectively extant—of a selfhood in a particular realm which includes and overrides the general, instead of being included in or overridden by it. This selfhood does not yet exist for contemporary man, but looms as a realisable possibility if man deliberately and successfully intervenes as one of the factors of his own destiny.

(*b*) As far as knowledge is concerned, the contemporary situation signifies the increasing accessibility of form and method, and of many of the elements of science, to a continually increasing number of persons. But as far as the individual is concerned, not only are the attainable limits very different from person to person—this being an objective matter—but also subjectively in most persons the will is not yet ripe, and hence they remain incapable of a spontaneous urge towards fundamental knowledge. From a generalised outlook upon knowledge it might be supposed that an identical situation would be possible for us all as the expression of comprehensive inter-communication which could readily determine the mental situation of all the human beings of a particular period after a uniform fashion. But this uniformity is rendered impossible by the discrepancies between us as regards desire for knowledge.

(c) Coming now to the relations between one self-hood and another, there is no generalisable situation, but only the absolute historicity of those who encounter one another, the intimacy of their contact, the fidelity and irreplaceability of personal ties. Amid the general social dissolution, man is thrust back into dependence upon these most primitive bonds, out of which alone a new and trustworthy objectivity can be constructed.

It is, then, incontestable that there can be no such thing as a homogeneous situation for all the human beings of a particular epoch. Were we to conceive the existence of mankind as a sort of unified substance which from age to age found itself in varying specific situations, the imagination would lose itself in the void. Even though, by a supposititious divine being, the process of human development might be regarded as proceeding in some such fashion, I as an individual should, however extensive my knowledge, run my course within the process, and could not as a cognitive being stand outside it. All the same, and apart from the three varieties of specific situations in their boundless interramifications, it is current usage to speak of the mental situation of the epoch as if such a situation actually existed. But here in our thought we come to a parting of the ways.

Assuming ourselves capable of adopting the outlook of a deity contemplating our existence from without, we can construct for ourselves an image of the whole. In the history of mankind we direct our gaze towards one particular point, that of the present. An objective entirety, whether clear-cut in its outlines as static, or nebulous because conceived as in process of becoming, is then the background upon which I cognitively project my situation in its inevitability, uniqueness, and mutability. My place is, as it were, determined by co-ordinates; what I am is a function of this place; existence is integral; and I myself am but a modification, or a consequence, or a link in the chain. My essence is the historical epoch and the sociological situation as a whole.

The historical picture of universal human development as a necessary process of one kind or another is doubtless fascinating. I am what the time is. But what the time is, discloses itself as a particular phase in the process. If I know this phase, I know what the time demands. To come to grips with existence, I must know the totality through knowing which I learn where we stand to-day. The tasks allotted to us in the present are to be fervently accepted as unconditionally incumbent on us in that present. They do, indeed, restrict me to the present, but insofar as I contemplate them in the present I simultaneously belong to the vast totality. No one can transcend the limitations of his epoch. If he should attempt to do so, he will merely fall into the void. Since I cognise the epoch through my cognition of the whole, or regard the cognition of the epoch as a desirable aim, I am confidently opposed to those who repudiate the demands of the epoch as I cognise it. To me they seem renegades, shirkers, defeatists, deserters from the cause of reality. They are traitors who have hauled down the flag!

Of course one who thinks in this way cannot escape the dread of being, after all, untimely, unseasonable. He watches anxiously lest he should be left behind, afraid that, while reality continues its steady march, he may fall out of step. The supreme question, therefore, is, what "the time demands". How delightful to be able to declare this, that, or the other to be pre-Kantian, old-fashioned, pre-war! With such phrases, a doom is sealed. Enough to say reproachfully: "You are behind the times; you are out of touch with realities; you fail to understand the new generation!" Only the new is the true; youth alone stands in the foremost front of time. Be up-to-date at any cost! Such an impulse towards contemporary self-assertion culminates in a trumpeting of the present, a glorification of the passing show—as if there could be no shadow of a doubt as to what the present really is.

But the opinion that we can know what the whole, historically or at this actual moment, really is, is fallacious. The very existence of the alleged whole is questionable. No matter whether I choose to regard the epoch as a spiritual principle, as a specific feeling of life, as a sociological structure, as a particular economic order or a particular system of government—in any case what I comprehend is not the ultimate origin of the whole, but merely one of a number of obtainable perspectives of orientation therein. I cannot possibly survey from without that entity which in no circumstances whatever I can leave. Since my own being has inevitably to play its part in the integrality of existence, independent knowledge is but a "pious wish": it is the sketch of a route I should like to follow; it is resentment which finds an outlet in the animus of such supposititious knowledge; it is passivity which is thereby justified; it is an æsthetic pleasure which I derive from the splendour of my imaginary picture; it is a gesture whereby I can gratify my self-assertive impulse.

Nonetheless, in the world of relativity, glimpses of the kind have a use and a meaning—are, indeed, indispensable if we are really to grasp our own situation when we come to venture upon the other and true path which knows naught of a totality. As soon as I have become aware how and by what means and within what limits knowledge is attainable, I have no choice but incessantly to strive towards an understanding of my time and its situations. A knowledge of my world provides the sole means whereby I can: first of all, become aware of the extent of the possible; secondly, shape sound plans and form effective resolves; thirdly, acquire the outlooks and the ideas that will enable me (a philosopher) to interpret human life as a manifestation of the transcendental.

Thus when I have entered upon the true path I am faced by the antinomy that my original impulse to comprehend the whole was foredoomed to shipwreck through the inevitable tendency of the whole to be shattered into fragments—into particular glimpses and constellations out of which, building in reverse order, I attempt to reconstruct a whole.

But to conceive these antitheses in too absolute a fashion would be a mistake. I assume the whole to be a thing cognised, and yet I have only a vague image of it; or I rest content in a particular perspective without having the remotest intention of seeking to cognise the whole, and I falsify the situation by regarding as absolute what is no more than contingent.

The two erroneous outlooks have something in common even though they are opposed. The vague image of the whole is a comfort to one who stands aloof and no longer directly co-operates, except through criticism or appraisement or enthusiastic hope, while deeming himself in mere converse with what is taking place without his participation. The fixation of a finite situation in the conviction that it is being-in-itself shuts the consciousness within the narrows of contingency. Images of the whole, on the one hand, and undue definiteness as regards particulars, on the other, contribute jointly to the sloth which enables a man to be satisfied with merely superficial activities, while never troubling himself with the endeavour to get to the bottom of things.

Contrasted with both is the attitude of mind which regards itself as selfhood trying to achieve orientation; the object of clarifying the situation being to comprehend as clearly and decisively as possible one's own development in the particular situation. Human existence cannot be wholly cognised either as past or as present. Contrasted with the real situation of the individual, every generally comprehended situation is an abstraction, and its description is no more than the description of a type. Measured by this standard there will be much that is lacking to the concrete situation, and much will be added which has no bearing upon definitive knowledge. But images of situations are spurs whereby the individual is stimulated to attempt to find his way to the root of what takes place.

4. WAYS OF THROWING LIGHT ON THE PRESENT SITUATION

The construction of the mental situation of the present (which is a process that will not lapse into the solidity of a completed stereoscopic image) will continue. With growing awareness of the limits of the knowable, on the one part, and of the risks of undue absoluteness, on the other, there will be a tendency to rest content with particular perspectives as representations of the situation. In their particularity they will be valid, but they will have no absolute validity.

If the life-order of the masses of mankind be regarded as the principle of reality, this principle ceases to apply when we reach the frontiers where nameless powers come to be regarded as decisive.

If the decay of mental activity be insisted on, that can only be up to the limits where new possibilities begin to disclose themselves.

If the specific feature of the time be found in the way in which people regard human existence, then our demonstration leads us to the point where the philosophy of human existence becomes transformed into existence-philosophy.

If a contemplative forecast be made, this can assuredly be with no other aim than to replace it in due course by an active forecast.

If we speak of life, our aim must be to make selfhood palpable.

Thus our consideration of the mental situation of the present moves in antitheses which do not contrast with one another on the same plane, but appear upon intersecting planes of thought. In the end, therefore, we do not know what is, but seek to know what can be.

Man cannot seek to know what the Godhead could know. Such knowledge would put an end to his existence in time, whose activities are the purpose of his knowledge.

PART ONE

LIMITS OF THE LIFE-ORDER

Owing to the turmoil of modern life, what is really happening eludes our comprehension. We are voyaging upon a uncharted sea, unable to reach a shore from which a clear outlook on the whole would be attainable. Or, to modify the image, we circle in a whirlpool which only discloses things to us because we are dragged along in its eddies.

It is not to-day taken as a matter of course that human life is the supply of mass-needs by rationalised production with the aid of technical advances. The assumption seems to be that the whole can be reduced to perfect order by reason alone. But if this knowledge of the entirety of a comprehensible process of human organisation of the world should advance to become a decisive awareness of the being of the present, then that being would be for us no longer an unfathomable maelstrom of utterly elusive possibilities, but would present itself as the necessary economic evolution of an apparatus currently at work.

However, the life-order is perpetually troubled; its decay seems imminent; it appears incapable of perfectionment. The question arises whether it can itself become the "whole" for us, or whether it is really no more than a part of an environing and overriding whole. The frontiers of the life-order disclose to us the State, mind, and humanity itself as the origins of human activity—as origins which do not enter into any life-order, although they are essential to making this order possible.

The way wherein man evokes his knowledge of reality out of these origins is what first, in combination with this reality, creates his mental situation. In order to elucidate this situation, we set out from the manner in which reality is contemplated to-day. A bare depiction of contemporary existence such as will prove acceptable to every one no matter what his political or philosophical outlook may be, will suffice to make it clear that a knowledge of the reality of man is not identical with that reality itself, although each throws the other into relief. The reality which manifests itself in apparently inevitable glimpses seems to show that man is entirely dependent; and yet what man himself becomes is the upshot of the way in which he elaborates the knowledge which the contemporary mental situation forces on him. Man is faced by the problem whether he will fatalistically submit to the sway of the mighty forces which appear to determine everything that happens, or whether, after all, paths are discernible along which he can walk freely because on them the writ of the aforesaid powers no longer runs.

1. TECHNIQUE AND APPARATUS AS DETERMINANTS OF MASS-LIFE

Estimates of the total population of the world are: for 1800, roughly 850 millions; for the present time, 1,800 millions. This unprecedented increase, whereby the population has been considerably more than doubled in four-thirds of a century, was rendered possible by technical advances. The results of discoveries and inventions were as follows: a new basis for production; the organization of enterprises; a methodical increase in the productivity of labour; a world-wide and enormous improvement in the means of transport and communication; the codification of law and the establishment of effective police systems, whereby public order was ensured; and, as the combined effect of all the foregoing, greatly improved facilities for anticipating the results of industrial and commercial enterprise. Huge undertakings can now be purposively guided from a single centre, even though their employees are numbered by the hundred thousand and their tentacles extend over the entire surface of the globe.

This development is associated with the rationalisation of productive and distributive activity, resolves being made in accordance with knowledge and calculation instead of mere instinct and desire; and it is likewise associated with mechanisation, all the work being done under detailed rules and regulations which apply to every one concerned. Whereas in such matters people used to wait upon events, and make no more until "something turned up", they now think things out beforehand and leave nothing to chance—with the result, however, that in many respects the individual worker becomes little more than a part of the machinery.

The broad masses of the population could not exist to-day but for the titanic interlocking wheelwork of which each worker is one of the cogs. Thereby our elementary needs are supplied with an efficiency new to history. As late as the beginning of the nineteenth century there were famines in Germany. Pestilences wrought havoc, infant mortality was terribly high, and very few persons lived to be old. To-day famine during peace-time is unknown in western civilised lands.   Whereas in 1750 the annual death-rate among the inhabitants of London was one in twenty, to-day it is one in eighty.   Thanks to insurance against illness and unemployment in conjunction with other social-welfare institutions, no one is nowadays left remorselessly exposed to the danger of death by starvation, as used to be the lot of whole sections of the European population.   In Asia, on the other hand, this risk is still regarded as a matter of course.

The supply of the masses with the necessaries of life is not effected in accordance with a unified plan, being the outcome of an enormously complicated system in which rationalisation and mechanisation bring together a mighty stream deriving from number-less sources.   The general result is not a slave-economy wherein human beings can be dealt with like the lower animals, but an economy of independent personalities, the good will and voluntary co-operation of each in his place being essential to the proper working of the whole.   Democracy in one form or another must, therefore, be the political structure of this apparatus.   No longer can anyone arbitrarily decide, in accordance with a preconceived plan, what the masses are to do; for popular approval or tolerance is now indispensable.   Substantially the working of the apparatus is the resultant of a vast number of individual voluntary tensions, which collaborate in the end despite reciprocal conflicts; and what the indi-vidual does is, in the long run, determined by his efficiency as a producer.   Thus, though all work is purposive, there is no purposive economy as a whole.

During the last two centuries the science of political economy has evolved upon the basis of this conception of the life-order.   Since technico-economic and social developments, as realised by the general consciousness, have come more and more to determine the historical course of events, a knowledge of these movements has tended to become the science of human affairs. That explains why the seemingly simple principle of a purposive and rational ordering of the provision of the elementary necessaries of human life has assumed so extraordinarily complicated an aspect. We are concerned here with regulation and control which are never visible as such in their integrality, and can only keep in being through incessant transformation.

2. MASS-RULE

The technical life-order and the masses are closely interrelated. The huge machinery of social provision must be adapted to the peculiarities of the masses; its functioning, to the amount of labour power available; its output, to the demands of the consumers. We infer, therefore, that the masses must rule, and yet we find that they cannot rule.

Peculiarities of the Masses. The term "masses" is ambiguous. If we mean an undifferentiated aggregate of contemporary persons in a particular situation and forming a unity because they are all under the stress of the same affects, it is plain that such an aggregate can only exist for a brief space of time. If we use the word "masses" as a synonym for the "public", this denotes a group of persons mentally interlinked by their common reception of certain opinions, but a group vague in its limits and its stratification, though at times a typical historical product. The "masses", however, as an aggregate of persons who are articulated in some apparatus of the life-order in such a manner that the will and the peculiarities of the majority among them are decisive, constitute the unceasingly operative and effective power in our world—the power which manifests itself no more than transiently in the "public" or in a "mob".

The peculiarities of the masses as the fleeting unity of a mob or crowd have been ably analysed by Gustav le Bon as impulsiveness, suggestibility, intolerance, and mutability. The "public" is a phantom, the phantom of an opinion supposed to exist in a vast number of persons who have no effective interrelation and though the opinion is not effectively present in the units. Such an opinion is spoken of as "public opinion", a fiction which is appealed to by individuals and by groups as supporting their special views. It is impalpable, illusory, transient; "'tis here, 'tis there, 'tis gone"; a nullity which can nevertheless for a moment endow the multitude with power to uplift or to destroy.

The peculiarities of the masses articulated in an apparatus are not uniform. The manual worker, the salaried employee, the doctor, the lawyer, do not as such combine to form the masses; each is a potential individual; but the proletariat, the general body of the medical profession, the teaching staff of a university—these respectively combine to form an articulated "mass" insofar as in actual fact the majority of the corporation decides the nature, the actions, the resolves of all its members. One might expect that the average qualities of human nature would everywhere prevail. What the "mass-man" on the average is, is disclosed in what most people do; in what is usually bought and consumed; in what one can generally expect when one has to deal with people "in the mass"—as apart from the "fads" of individuals. Just as the budget of a private household throws light upon the tastes of the members of that household, so does the budget of a State (to the extent that the majority decides) disclose the tastes of the bulk of its citizens. If we know how much money an individual has to spend, we can infer his peculiarities when he tells us "I cannot afford this, but I can afford that." Contact with many persons teaches us what, on the average, we can expect from them. For millenniums, judgments in these respects have been remarkably similar. People "in the mass" would seem to be guided by the search for pleasure and to work only under the crack of the whip or when impelled by a craving for bread and for dainties; yet they are bored when they have nothing to do, and have a perpetual craving for novelty.

An articulated mass, however, has other qualities than these. In that sense there is no "mass" of all mankind; there are only diverse masses which form, dissolve, and reform. The corporations which, by tranquil efficiency or by organised voting, decide what shall happen, are articulated masses when within each of them the individual counts only as a unit among many having like powers. Yet these articulated masses are mutable, diversified, transitory expressions of some specific historical outcome of human existence. Articulated masses can, however, express themselves at times in other than average ways, showing themselves capable on these occasions of the unusual. Although as a rule the mass is stupider and less cultivated than the individual, in exceptional instances it may excel the individual in shrewdness and profundity.

Importance of the Masses. Man as member of a mass is no longer his isolated self. The individual is merged in the mass, to become something other than he is when he stands alone. On the other hand in the mass the individual becomes an isolated atom whose individual craving to exist has been sacrificed, since the fiction of a general equality prevails. Yet each individual continues to say to himself: "What another has, I also want; what another can do, I also can do." In secret, therefore, envy persists, and so does the longing to enjoy by having more and being of more importance than others.

This inevitable mass-effect is intensified to-day by the complicated articulations of a modern economic society. The rule of the masses affects the activities and habits of the individual. It has become obligatory to fulfil a function which shall in some way be regarded as useful to the masses. The masses and their apparatus are the object of our most vital interest. The masses are our masters; and for every one who looks facts in the face his existence has become dependent on them, so that the thought of them must control his doings, his cares, and his duties. He may despise them in their average aspects; or he may feel that the solidarity of all mankind is destined some day to become a reality; or he may, while not denying the responsibility which each man has for all, still hold more or less aloof: but it remains a responsibility he can never evade. He belongs to the masses, though they threaten to let him founder amid rhetoric and the commotions of the multitude. Even an articulated mass always tends to become unspiritual and inhuman. It is life without existence, superstition without faith. It may stamp all flat; it is disinclined to tolerate independence and greatness, but prone to constrain people to become as automatic as ants.

When the titanic apparatus of the mass-order has been consolidated, the individual has to serve it, and must from time to time combine with his fellows in order to renovate it. If he wants to make his livelihood by intellectual activity, he will find it very difficult to do this except by satisfying the needs of the many. He must give currency to something that will please the crowd. They seek satisfaction in the pleasures of the table, eroticism, self-assertion; they find no joy in life if one of these gratifications be curtailed. They also desire some means of self-knowledge. They desire to be led in such a way that they can fancy themselves leaders. Without wishing to be free, they would fain be accounted free. One who would please their taste must produce what is really average and commonplace, though not frankly styled such; must glorify or at least justify something as universally human. Whatever is beyond their understanding is uncongenial to them.

One who would influence the masses must have recourse to the art of advertisement. The clamour of puffery is to-day requisite even for an intellectual movement. The days of quiet and unpretentious activity seem over and done with. You must keep yourself in the public eye, give lectures, make speeches, arouse a sensation. Yet the mass-apparatus lacks true greatness of representation, lacks solemnity. No one believes in festal celebrations, not even the participants. In the Middle Ages, the Pope sometimes made a quasi-royal progress through Europe; but we can hardly conceive such a thing to-day in (let us suppose) the United States, the present chief centre of world-power. The Americans would not take the successor of St. Peter seriously!

3. THE TENSION BETWEEN TECHNICAL MASS-ORDER AND HUMAN LIFE

Limits are imposed upon the life-order by a specifically modern conflict. The mass-order brings into being a universal life-apparatus, which proves destructive to the world of a truly human life.

Man lives as part of a social environment to which he is bound by remembered and prospective ties. Men do not exist as isolated units, but as members of a family in the home; as friends in a group; as parts of this, that, or the other "herd" with well-known historical origins. He has become what he is thanks to a tradition which enables him to look back into the obscurity of his beginnings and makes him responsible for his own future and that of his associates. Only in virtue of a long view before and after does he acquire a substantial tenure in that world which he constructs out of his heritage from the past. His daily life is permeated by the spirit of a perceptibly present world which, however small, is still something other than himself. His inviolable property is a narrow space, the ownership of which enables him to share in the totality of human history.

The technical life-order which came into being for the supply of the needs of the masses did at the outset preserve these real worlds of human creatures, by furnishing them with commodities. But when at length the time in which nothing in the individual's immediate and real environing world was any longer made, shaped, or fashioned by that individual for his own purposes; when everything that came, came merely as the gratification of momentary need, to be used up and cast aside; when the very dwelling-place was machine-made, when the environment had become despiritualised, when the day's work grew sufficient to itself and ceased to be built up into a constituent of the worker's life—then man was, as it were, bereft of his world. Cast adrift in this way, lacking all sense of historical continuity with past or future, man cannot remain man. The universalisation of the life-order threatens to reduce the life of the real man in a real world to a mere functioning in the void.

But man as individual refuses to allow himself to be absorbed into a life-order which would only leave him in being as a function for the maintenance of the whole. True, he can live in the apparatus with the aid of a thousand relationships on which he is dependent and in which he collaborates; but since he has become a mere replaceable cog in a wheelwork regardless of his individuality, he rebels if there is no other way in which he can manifest his selfhood.

If, however, he wants to "be himself", if he craves for self-expression, there promptly arises a tension between his self-preservative impulse, on the one hand, and his real selfhood, on the other. Immediate self-will is what primarily moves him, for he is animated by a blind desire for the advantages attendant on making good in the struggle for life. Yet the urge to self-expression drives him into incalculable hazards which may render his means of livelihood perilously insecure. Under stress of these two conflicting impulses he may act in ways which will interfere with the tranquil and stable functioning of the life-order. Consequently the disturbance of the life-order has its permanent antinomy in a twofold possibility. Inasmuch as self-will provides the space wherein selfhood can realise itself as existence, the former is as it were the body of the latter, and may drag the latter down to ruin or (in favourable circumstances) bring it to fruition.

If, then, self-will and existence both seek a world for themselves, they come into conflict with the universal life-order. But this, in its turn, strives to gain mastery over the powers which are threatening its frontiers. It is, therefore, profoundly concerned about matters which are not directly contributory to the self-preservative impulse. This latter, which can be indifferently regarded as a vital need for obtaining the necessaries of life and as an existential absolute, may be termed the "non-rational". When thus negatively conceived, it is degraded to a being of the second order: but it is either promoted once more to the first rank within certain restricted provinces; or else, in contrast with purely rational aims, it may acquire a positive interest, as in love, adventure, sport, and play. Or, again, it may be resisted as undesirable, this being what we see in those who are affected with a dread of life or a lack of joy in work. Thus in one or other of these ways it is diverted into the decisively and exclusively vital field—to the denial of the claim to existence slumbering within it. The powers interested in the functioning of the apparatus, in the paralysing of the masses, in the individual mind, seek to further the demands of the self-preservative impulse as a non-committal gratification, and to deprive it of its possible absoluteness. By rationalising the non-rational, in order to re-establish it as a kind of gratification of elementary needs, the attempt is made to achieve that which is not genuinely possible. The result is that what was originally fostered as something other than it is, is destroyed by what seems to be an endeavour to care for it. A prey to technical dominance, it assumes a grey tint or a crude motley coloration, wherein man no longer recognises himself, being robbed of his individuality as a human creature. Yet, since it is uncontrollable, it rides rough-shod over the ordinances formulated to destroy it.

The claim to self-will and to existence [to self-expression] cannot be abrogated—any more than there is a possibility, once the masses have come into being, of dispensing with the need for a universal apparatus as an essential condition for the life and welfare of every individual. Tension between the universal life-apparatus and a truly human world is, therefore, inevitable. Each is endowed with its reality only in virtue of the other; and were one to effect a definitive conquest of the other, it would thereby instantly destroy itself. Attempted mastery and attempted revolt will continue their reciprocal strike, each misunderstanding the other, though each fruitfully stimulates the other. Mutual misunderstanding is unavoidable because of the conflict between the self-preservative impulse as a vital urge and existence [the craving for higher forms of self-expression] in its absoluteness.

The limits to the life-order will everywhere become manifest where man grows fully aware of himself.

What has made life as we now live it possible, and what is therefore indispensable, is nevertheless a danger to man's selfhood. The growth of knowledge during the era of advanced technique in conjunction with the spreading dominion of apparatus seem to narrow man's potentialities even while enriching him. It is obvious that he may founder if, as is possible, no efficient leaders appear upon the scene. A symbol of the world in which, somehow or other, so long as he remains man, he has to live, a symbol of the world which is his necessary historical environment, is the life of the home. The fact that he knows himself menaced is shown by his dread of life; the fact that he can secure self-expression in his daily achievement is shown by (when he has it) joy in work; and the way in which he realises his vital reality is disclosed in sport.

Consciousness during the Era of Advanced Technique.
The upshot of technical advances as far as everyday
life is concerned has been that there is a trustworthy
supply of necessaries, but in a way which makes us
take less pleasure in them, because they come to us
as a matter of course instead of with the relish given
by a sense of positive fulfilment. Being mere materials
obtainable at a moment's notice in exchange for money,
they lack the aroma of that which is produced by
personal effort. Articles of consumption are supplied
in the mass and are used up, their refuse being thrown
away; they are readily interchangeable, one specimen
being as good as another. In manufactured articles
turned out in large quantities, no attempt is made to
achieve a unique and precious quality, to produce
something whose individuality makes it transcend
fashion, something that will be carefully cherished.
An article which thus satisfies ordinary needs arouses
no peculiar sense of affection, and is only felt to be
important if it should chance to be unobtainable. In
that last respect, certainly, a general security of provision, growing ever more extensive, intensifies the
emotions of want and danger should anything go
wrong with the supply.

Among articles of consumption we distinguish the
well-adapted and substantially perfected kinds, the
definitive forms whose manufacture has become
thoroughly normalised. Such commodities have not
sprung completely finished from one exceptional brain,
but are the outcome of successive discoveries and
improvements that have continued, perhaps, for more
than a generation. The bicycle, for instance, took
twenty years to pass through the various stages of its
revolution (some of which now look to us more than a
little comic) before attaining finality in a restricted

number of minor varieties. Although the majority of articles of consumption still repel in one way or another by inelegancies of form, by errors of excess or defect, by unpracticalness in matters of detail, by maladaptations in point of technique, or what not, the ideal shines forth, and in a fair number of instances has been attained. When perfectionment has gone as far as this, fondness for a particular specimen has become unmeaning. The general form is what matters to us, and, however artificial that may be, such things have a functional suitability which almost makes them seem like natural products rather than the creatures of man's activity.

Thanks to the technical conquest of time and space by the daily press, modern travel, the cinema, wireless, etc., a universalisation of contact has become possible. No longer is anything remote, mysterious, wonderful. All can participate as witnesses of events accounted great or important. Persons who occupy leading positions are as well known to us as if we rubbed shoulders with them day by day.

The attitude of mind characteristic of this world of advanced technique has been termed positivism. The positivist does not want phrase-making, but knowledge; not ponderings about meaning, but dextrous action; not feelings, but objectivity; not a study of mysterious influences, but a clear ascertainment of facts. Reports of what has been observed must be given concisely, plastically, without sentimentalism. An aggregate of disjointed data, even sound ones, producing the effect of being the relics of earlier education, are worth nothing. Constructive thought is demanded, rather than the making of many words; simplicity and directness, rather than eloquence. Control and organisation are supreme,

The matter-of-factness of the technical realm makes its familiars skilled in their dealings with all things; the ease with which ideas about such matters are communicated, standardises knowledge; hygiene and comfort schematise bodily and erotic life. Daily affairs are carried on in conformity with fixed rules. The desire to act in accordance with general conventions, to avoid startling any one by the unusual, results in the establishment of a typical behaviour which reconstructs upon a new plane something akin to the rule of taboos in primitive times.

The individual is merged in the function. Being is objectified, for positivism would be violated if individuality remained conspicuous. The individual consciousness is absorbed into the social, so that, in exceptional instances, the individual has joy in work without any tinge of selfishness. It is the collectivity that matters; and what to the individual would be tedious, nay intolerable, becomes endurable to him as part of the collectivity, in which a new stimulus inspires him. He exists only as "we".

Essential humanity is reduced to the general; to vitality as a functional corporeality, to the triviality of enjoyment. The divorce of labour from pleasure deprives life of its possible gravity: public affairs become mere entertainment; private affairs, the alternation of stimulation and fatigue, and a craving for novelty whose inexhaustible current flows swiftly into the waters of oblivion. There is no continuity, only pastime. Positivism likewise encourages an unceasing activity of the impulses common to us all: an enthusiasm for the numberless and the vast, for the creations of modern technique, for huge crowds; sensational admiration for the achievements, fortunes, and abilities of outstanding individuals; the complication and brutalisation of the erotic; gambling, adventurousness, and even the hazarding of one's life. Lottery tickets are sold by the million; crossword puzzles become the chief occupation of people's leisure. This positive gratification of the mind without personal participation or effort promotes efficiency for the daily round, fatigue and recreation being regularised.

In becoming a mere function, life forfeits its historical particularity, to the extreme of a levelling of the various ages of life. Youth as the period of highest vital efficiency and of erotic exaltation becomes the desired type of life in general. Where the human being is regarded only as a function, he must be young; and if youth is over, he will still strive to show its semblance. Add to this that, for primary reasons, age no longer counts. The individual's life is experienced only momentarily, its temporal extension being a chance duration, not remembered and cherished as the upbuilding of irrevocable decisions upon the foundation of biological phases. Since a human being no longer has any specific age, he is always simultaneously at the beginning and the end; he can do now this, now that, and now the other; everything seems at any moment possible, and yet nothing truly real. The individual is no more than one instance among millions; why then should he think his doings of any importance? What happens, happens quickly and is soon forgotten. People therefore tend to behave as if they were all of the same age. Children become like grown-ups as soon as they possibly can, and join in grown-up conversations on their own initiative. When the old pretend to be young, of course the young have no reverence for their elders. These latter, instead of (as they should) keeping the young at a distance and setting them a standard, assume the airs of an invincible vitality, such as beseems youth but is unbecoming to age. Genuine youth wants to maintain its disparity, and not to be mingled without distinction among elders. Age wants form and realisation and the continuity of its destiny.

Since positivism makes a general demand for simplicity that shall render things universally comprehensible, it tends towards establishing a sort of "universal language" for the expression of all modes of human behaviour. Not merely fashions, but rules for social intercourse, gestures, phrases, methods of conveying information, incline towards uniformity. There is now a conventional ethic of association: courteous smiles, a tranquil manner, the avoidance of haste and jostle, the adoption of a humorous attitude in strained situations, helpfulness unless the cost be unreasonable, the feeling that "personal remarks" are in bad taste, self-discipline to promote order and easy relationships whenever people are assembled in large numbers. All these things are advantageous to a multifariously communal life, and are actually achieved.

Dominion of Apparatus. Inasmuch as the titanic apparatus for the provision of the elementary necessaries of human life reduces the individual to a mere function, it releases him from the obligation to conform to the traditional standards which of old formed the cement of society. It has been said that in modern times men have been shuffled together like grains of sand. They are elements of an apparatus in which they occupy now one location, now another; not parts of a historical substance which they imbue with their selfhood. The number of those who lead this uprooted sort of life is continually on the increase. Driven from pillar to post, then perhaps out-of-work for a lengthy period with nothing more than bare subsistence, they no longer have a definite place or status in the whole. The profound saying that every one ought to have his own niche, to fulfil his proper task in the scheme of creation, has for them become a lying phrase, used in the futile endeavour to console persons who feel themselves adrift and forsaken. What a man can do nowadays can only be done by one who takes short views. He has occupation, indeed, but his life has no continuity. What he does is done to good purpose, but is then finished once for all. The task may be repeated after the same fashion many times, but it cannot be repeated in such an intimate way as to become, one might say, part of the personality of the doer; it does not lead to an expansion of the selfhood. What has been done, no longer counts, but only that which is actually being done. Oblivion is the basis of such a life, whose outlooks upon past and present shrink so much that scarcely anything remains in the mind but the bald present. Thus life flows on its course devoid of memories and foresights, lacking the energy derivable from a purposive and abstract outlook upon the part played in the apparatus. Love for things and human beings wanes and disappears. The machine-made products vanish from sight as soon as made and consumed, all that remains in view being the machinery by which new commodities are being made. The worker at the machine, concentrating upon immediate aims, has no time or inclination left for the contemplation of life as a whole.

When the average functional capacity has become the standard of achievement, the individual is regarded with indifference. No one is indispensable. He is not himself, having no more genuine individuality than one pin in a row, a mere object of general utility. Those most effectively predestined to such a life are persons without any serious desire to be themselves. Such have the preference. It seems as if the world must be given over to mediocrities, to persons without a destiny, without a rank or a difference, without genuinely human attributes.

It is as if the man thus deracinated and reduced to the level of a thing, had lost the essence of humanity. Nothing appeals to him with the verity of substantial being. Whether in enjoyment or discomfort, whether strenuous or fatigued, he is still nothing more than the function of his daily task. As he lives on from day to day, the only desire that may stir him beyond that of performing this task is the desire to occupy the best obtainable place in the apparatus. The mass of those who stay in their appointed situations becomes segregated from those who ruthlessly press forward. The former are passive, remain where they are, and amuse themselves in their leisure hours; the latter are active, being spurred on by ambition and the will to power, consumed as with fire by the thought of the chances of promotion, by the tensing of their utmost energies.

The whole apparatus is guided by a bureaucracy, which is itself likewise an apparatus—human beings reduced to apparatus, one upon which all those at work in the greater apparatus are dependent. The State, the municipality, manufacturing and business enterprises, are controlled by bureaucracies. To-day men are associated for labour in multitudes, and their work must be organised. Those who force a way into the front ranks have secured advancement and enjoy higher consideration; but essentially they, too, are the slaves of their functions, which merely demand an alerter intelligence, a more specialised talent, and a more lively activity than those of the crowd.

The dominion of apparatus is favourable to persons equipped with the faculties which will thus bring them to the front: is advantageous to far-seeing and relentless individuals who are well-acquainted with the qualities of average human beings and are therefore able to manage them efficiently, who are ready and willing to acquire expertise in some department or other, who can strive unrestingly without concern for anything but the main chance, and who are sleeplessly possessed by the thought of getting on in the world.

There are further requisites. The would-be climber must be able to make himself liked. He must persuade, and at times even corrupt—be serviceable enough to make himself indispensable—be able to hold his tongue, to circumvent, to lie a little though not too much—be indefatigable in the discovery of reasons—ostensibly modest—have a readiness to appeal to sentiment on occasions—be capable of working in a manner that will please his superiors—avoid showing independence except in those matters wherein independence is expected of him by his chiefs.

Where scarcely any one is born to command and therefore educated to command, and where a high position in the apparatus has to be climbed up to by the aspirant, this acquirement of a leading situation is dependent upon behaviour, instincts, valuations, which imperil true selfhood as a determinant of responsible leadership. Luck and chance may sometimes bring about advancement. Speaking generally, however, the winners in the race have qualities which disincline them to allow others to be their true selves. Hence the winners tend to snub all those who aim at adequate self-expression, speaking of them as pre-

tentious, eccentric, biased, unpractical, and measuring
their achievements by insincere absolute standards;
they are personally suspect, they are stigmatised as
provocative, as disturbers of the peace, as people who
kick over the traces.   Because he only "arrives" who
has sacrificed his selfhood, the arrivist will not tolerate
self-expression in subordinates.

Consequently peculiar methods of advancement in
the apparatus decide the choice among the candidates
for high places.   Because no one gets on who does
not thrust himself forward, and yet to be "pushing"
is considered bad form in any particular case, the convention is that the candidate must ostensibly wait till
he is summoned; and the problem each has to solve
is how to thrust himself into a position while seeming
indifferent to promotion.   A rumour is started inconspicuously, in casual conversation.   Hypotheses are
mooted with an air of indifference.   The ball is opened
by some such phrase as: "I am not really thinking of";
or, "it is hardly to be expected that", etc.   If nothing
comes of the suggestion, no harm has been done.   If,
on the other hand, it bears fruit, one can soon begin
talking of a concrete proposal, declare that an offer
has been made, and bruit it abroad that nothing was
farther from one's mind than any such expectation.
One can even feign reluctance.   The aspirant accus-
toms himself to being double-faced and double-
tongued.   He will enter into as many promising
relationships as possible, so that he may be able to
turn some of them to useful account.   Instead of the
comradeship of persons all of whom are their genuine
selves, we have the spurious friendship of a gang
whose motto is "You scratch my back and I'll scratch
yours."   The important thing is not to be a spoil-
sport when pleasure is afoot; to be outwardly respect-

ful to all; to show indignation when one is sure that others will do the same; to join in log-rolling to the common advantage—and so on.

Leadership. Were it possible that the development of the universal life-order should proceed so far as to absorb the whole world of human beings as individuals, the final upshot for man would be self-extinction. In that case the apparatus, even, would have destroyed itself, through destroying the men without which it cannot continue to exist. True organisation can assign to each his function, the amount he shall work and the amount he shall consume; but it cannot engender its own leader. The ordinary unreflective person will only do his utmost under conditions which leave nothing to his own initiative, and where no call is made upon him to think for himself. He must work in an aggregate which, so far as he is concerned, exists in and by itself. Harnessed in an apparatus directed by an alien will, he obediently does the work that is assigned to him. If any sort of decision is demanded of him, it is taken haphazard within the limited province of his function, without his having to probe to the bottom of things. Difficulties are smoothed out of his path by the rules and regulations laid down for his guidance, or by the resignation with which he blindly obeys orders. But a genuine and world-creative community of action can be achieved only when he who issues orders does so with a thorough sense of responsibility, and when he who obeys understands thoroughly the reasons for what he is doing; only, in a word, among persons who are truly themselves; only when the leader is acquainted with the few upon whose independent judgment he can rely, to join with them in following the inner voice. Where, on the other hand, the apparatus has become all in all, and there is no longer any risk that success or failure shall imply a judgment upon the doers, no further scope is left for initiative. Yet even while the apparatus demands work devoid of initiative, this work can only thrive so long as, at crucial points, there are leaders who have established their position by merging themselves in their world. If, in days to come, such persons are lacking (because from youth upwards they have been deprived of opportunities for self-development), then the apparatus itself will break down. The independence of self-expressive persons which at the frontiers of the apparatus was a danger to its smooth working, proves, after all, indispensable for a proper functioning in the course of its inevitable transformation.

Thus under mass-rule and under the dominion of apparatus, the importance of the individual leader persists, but peculiar circumstances now become decisive in the choice of leaders. Great men pass into the background as contrasted with the efficient. The apparatus which provides the necessaries of life for the masses is throughout served and guided by persons whose full understanding of the part they are playing is an essential factor in promoting the success of the whole. The power of the masses remains effective through the instrumentality of mass-organisations, majorities, public opinion, and the actual behaviour of vast multitudes of men. Yet this power only operates insofar as, from time to time, one individual or another makes the masses understand what they really want, and functions as their representative. Although in the apparatus there seldom appears a leader whose personal aims harmonise with the requirements of a huge aggregate of lives, and who is thus able to maintain his position while incessantly working for the general advantage, such leaders are requisite now and again, and "the right man in the right place" sometimes crops up as if by chance. Through the force of circumstances he has become temporarily indispensable. But ultimate power remains in the hands of the masses, for their assent is needed, even though in exceptional and temporary circumstances an individual has to decide. If, however, that individual can only reach this influential position through being brought up to be the functionary of the masses and through having always turned an attentive ear to their wishes, he will have his nature thus attuned, and will never run counter to their demands. He will regard himself, not as one endowed with independent selfhood, but merely as an exponent of the multitude which backs him up. At bottom he is as important as any other individual, the executant of whatever may be re-echoed by the average will of the masses. Without the support of the mass-will, he is of no account. What he can be is not measured by an ideal, is not related to a genuinely present transcendental, but is based upon his conception of the fundamental qualities of mankind as manifested in the majority and as dominant in action. Now, the result of "leadership" of this sort is inextricable confusion. At the parting of the ways in the life-order, where the question is between new creation or decay, that man will be decisive for new creation who is able on his own initiative to seize the helm and steer a course of his own choosing—even if that course be opposed to the will of the masses. Should the emergence of such persons become impossible, a lamentable shipwreck will be inevitable.

In the mass-organisation, dominion or leadership assumes a wraith-like invisibility. Some talk of

abolishing leadership altogether. [*A bas les chefs!*]
Those who raise this cry are blind to the fact that
without leadership, without rule, there could be no
life for the masses of mankind. It is because of the
lack of efficient leadership that disintegration, window-
dressing, and jiggery-pokery of all kinds are rife;
that unsavoury bargaining, procrastination, compromise, ill-considered decisions, and humbug are so
common. Everywhere on occasions we encounter
peculiar forms of corruption dependent upon self-
seeking and the pursuit of private advantage. They
continue because they are tacitly accepted by all concerned. If some flagrant instance be made public,
there is a transient commotion; but the hubbub soon
ceases owing to the general recognition that the
scandal is no more than a symptom of a deep-seated
malady.

Rare are those willing to shoulder responsibility.
Leaders whom chance has brought to the front seldom
decide anything without endorsement. They refuse
to move unless supported by some committee or con-
clave, and each of them tries to shift the onus upon
another. In the background, as ultimate court of
appeal, stands the massed authority of the people,
which seems to hold sway through the process of
election. But what really exists in this matter is
neither the rule of the masses as a corporation, nor
yet the freedom of individuals left to fulfil their
responsibilities as they think fit. We have, instead,
the authority of a method or system which is held
consecrate because it is reputed to promote the general
interest—and it is upon this method or system in
one of its multifarious forms that responsibility in the
last resort accrues. Each individual is a tiny wheel
with a fractional share in the decision, but no one

effectively decides. Only in this sense are people practical politicians, that things are first allowed to run their own course, and then intervention is restricted to the sanctioning of blindly-evolving reality. Sometimes an individual acquires exceptional powers; but, since he has not been prepared for this position by life in an aggregate, he is only competent, in the chance-developed situation, to use these powers for private interests or in accordance with doctrinaire theories. Whoever becomes conspicuous to the public is an object for sensationalism. The masses exult or get enraged when nothing decisive has taken place. Men will continue to wander aimlessly in a fog unless in relation to the general life-order there should, from some other source, appear and prevail man's own will to rule.

The Life of the Home. The home, the family community, is an outgrowth of the affection whereby the individual is bound to other members of that community in ties of lifelong fidelity. Its aim is to bring up children in such a way as to incorporate them into the traditional substance of the society to which they belong, thus facilitating the perpetual intercommunication which only amid the difficulties of daily life can achieve unrestrained realisation.

Herein we discern the most essential elements of our common humanity, and the foundation of all the others. Among the masses this primary humankindliness is unwittingly diffused, wholly self-dependent, linked in each case to its own little world with a destiny set apart from that of kindred microcosms. That is why to-day the importance of marriage has become greater than ever—for it was less in earlier days when public spirit was at a higher level and was a more fruitful source of general stability. To-day man has been, after a fashion, thrust back into the narrow space of his origins, there to decide whether he will continue to exist as man.

The family needs its domicile, its life-order, solidarity, mutual regard, trustworthiness on the part of all those who, by reciprocal obligations, secure a firm standing-ground therein.

Even now, people cling to this primitive world with invincible tenacity; but the tendencies to disintegrate it increase proportionally with the trend to render a universal life-order absolute.

Let us deal first with externals. The herding of the masses in houses that resemble barracks, the transformation of what should be a home into a mere lair or sleeping-place, and the increasing technicisation of daily life, tend to make people utterly indifferent to an environment which they change light-heartedly, no longer regarding it as something to which they are attached by strong spiritual ties. Powers that profess to be working in the interest of a wider and greater community, foster individual selfishness at the cost of the family and do their utmost to set children against the home. Public education, instead of being looked upon as nothing more than a supplement to education in the home, is now considered more important than the latter, and the ultimate aim grows manifest—to take children away from their parents so that they may develop into children of the community alone. People are no longer horrified at divorce, at the indulgence of polygamous inclinations, at the procurement of abortion, at homosexuality, and at suicide. This horror used to safeguard the family. Now such transgressions are lightly regarded; or if condemned, condemned at most in a pharisaical spirit; or indifferently adopted as part of the mass-ethic. In other cases we find that, by a heedless reaction, the condemnation of abortion and homosexuality is exclusively embodied in criminal codes, to which (being moral offences) they do not rightly belong.

These tendencies towards the break-up of the home are all the more menacing since they arise, through an inevitable development, out of the very being of the individuals who are to be found in family groups, those islands which still stand firm against the stream of the universal life-order. Marriage is one of the most thorny problems which contemporary man has to handle. It is impossible to foresee how many persons will be found constitutionally incompetent for the task. Numerous, beyond question, will be those who, losing that contact with the public and authoritative spirit which is necessary to their selfhood, will plunge into fathomless waters. It has further to be remembered that marriage has of late been rendered more difficult by the emancipation of woman and the growth of her economic independence, so that there is now an enormous supply of unmarried women ready and willing to gratify the sexual desires of the male. In many instances marriage is at best a contract, a breach of which on the part of the husband will entail only the conventional punishment of alimony. Increasing licence is attended by a demand for the facilitation of divorce. A sign of the disruption of connubial ties is the multiplication of books on marriage.

In view of this disorder, it has become the aim of the universal life-order to re-establish order in a domain where order can only be achieved by the individual through freedom and in consequence of the essential worth of his being, enlightened by education. Because erotic indulgence has been tending to loosen all ties, the rationalised life-order has endeavoured to master this perilous non-rationality. Even the sexual life is being technicised by the prescriptions of hygiene and all kinds of regulations for its skilful management, that it may become as pleasurable and free from conflicts as possible. Such a book as Van de Velde's *Ideal Marriage*, aiming as it does at the sexualisation of the conjugal union, is symptomatic of our time and of the attempt to rob the non-rational of its sting. We cannot but regard as significant the fact that in the prospectus of this work even Catholic theologians are found to recommend it. Both by the religious degradation of marriage to a life of the second order (a life which only by ecclesiastical sanction can be saved from the stigma of unchastity), and by the technicisation of love as a dangerous non-rationality, is the unconditionality that realises itself in marriage involuntarily but radically denied. Religion and technique here join forces unaware, in a campaign against love as the foundation of marriage. Thus regarded, marriage has no need of legitimation, for, being of existential origin, it has the unconditionality of life-determining fidelity—which will perhaps only ensure erotic happiness for casual moments. Love which is assured of itself solely through the freedom of existence has absorbed eroticism into itself, without degrading it and without recognising its lustful demands.

He who has jettisoned the ties of family and selfhood instead of developing them from their roots into an aggregate, can only live in the anticipated but ever-elusive spirit of the mass. If I do this, I fix my eyes on the universal life-order in the endeavour to attain everything thereby, while betraying my own true world and abandoning my claim to it. The home crumbles when I no longer confide in it, living only as class and as community of interests and as function in an enterprise, and pushing whithersoever I think that power inheres. What is only attainable through the whole does not absolve me from the demand that I should also effectively undertake such things as are primarily attainable through my own initiative.

The limit to the universal life-order is, therefore, imposed by the freedom of the individual who must (if human beings are to remain human beings) evoke from his own self that which no other can evoke from him.

Dread of Life. In the rationalisation and universalisation of the life-order there has grown contemporaneously with its fantastic success an awareness of imminent ruin tantamount to a dread of the approaching end of all that makes life worth living. Not only does the apparatus seem, by its perfectionment, to threaten the annihilation of everything; even the apparatus itself is menaced. A paradox results. Man's life has become dependent upon the apparatus which proves ruinous to mankind at one and the same time by its perfectionment and by its breakdown.

The prospect of so disastrous a future inspires the individual with dread, seeing that he cannot be content to become a simple function detached from his origin. A dread of life perhaps unparalleled in its intensity is modern man's sinister companion. He is alarmed at the likelihood that he will in the near future become unable to obtain the vital necessaries. Seeing their supply thus imperilled, his attention becomes riveted on them more strongly than ever before; and he is also inspired with a very different dread, namely that concerning his selfhood, which he cannot face up to.

Dread attaches itself to everything. All uncertainties are tinged by it unless we succeed in forgetting it. Care makes us unable to protect our lives adequately. The cruelties that used to abound everywhere without remark are less frequent than of yore, but we have become aware of those that remain and they seem more terrible than ever. He who wants to keep himself alive must strain his labour power to the uttermost; must work unrestingly, and subject to ever more intensive compulsion. Every one knows that a man who is left behind in the race will fall and remain untended; and he who has passed the age of forty feels that the world has no longer any use for him. True, we have our social-welfare institutions, our systems of social insurance, savings banks, and what not; but what public assistance and private charity can supply, falls more and more below what is regarded as the standard of a decent existence, even though people are no longer allowed to starve to death.

The dread of life attaches itself to the body. Although what statisticians term the expectation of life is considerably increased, we all have a growing sense of vital insecurity. People demand medical treatment far beyond what is regarded as reasonable from the medical and scientific point of view. If a man comes to look upon his life as spiritually unacceptable, as intolerable were it merely because he can no longer understand its significance, he takes flight into illness, which envelops him like a visible protector. For in those limitary situations which (as mere life-experiences) crush him inwardly, man needs, either the selfhood of freedom, or else some objective point of support.

Dread or anxiety increases to such a pitch that the sufferer may feel himself to be nothing more than a lost point in empty space, inasmuch as all human relationships appear to have no more than a temporary validity. The work that binds human beings into a community is of fleeting duration. In erotic relationships, the question of duty is not even raised. The sufferer from anxiety has confidence in no one; he will not enter into absolute ties with any other person. One who fails to participate in what others are doing is left alone. The threat of being sacrificed arouses the sense of having been utterly forsaken, and this drives the sufferer out of his frivolous ephemeralness into cynical hardness and then into anxiety. In general, life seems full of dread.

Anxiety interferes with the working of the various institutions which exist, as part of the life-order, to tranquillise people and make them forget. The organisations in question are designed to arouse a sense of membership. The apparatus promises safety to its members. Doctors try and talk the sick or those who believe themselves sick out of the fear of death. But these institutions function effectively only when things are going well with the individual. The life-order cannot dispel the dread which is part of every individual's lot. This anxiety can only be controlled by the more exalted dread felt by existence threatened with the loss of its selfhood, which induces an overriding religious or philosophical exaltation. When existence is paralysed, the dread of life cannot fail to grow. The all-embracing dominion of the life-order would destroy man as existence without ever being able to free him from the dread of life. It is, indeed, the tendency of the life-order to become absolute which arouses an uncontrollable dread of life.

The Problem of Joy in Work. Self-seeking and wilfulness are at their minimum in that joy in work without which the individual ultimately becomes paralysed. Consequently the maintenance of joy in work has become one of the fundamental problems in the world of technique. From time to time and momentarily its urgency is realised—and then the riddle is thrust aside. Permanently and for all members of the community it is essentially unsoluble.

Wherever people are reduced to the position of those who merely have to perform an allotted task, the problem of the cleavage between being a· human creature and being a worker plays a decisive part in the individual's fate. One's own life acquires a new preponderance, and joy in work grows relative. The apparatus forces this kind of life upon an ever-increasing number of persons.

To ensure the means of life for all, however, there must remain professions in which work cannot simply be allotted and performed under instructions; in which the actual achievement cannot possibly be measured adequately by objective standards. The work of the physician, the schoolmaster, the clergyman, etc., cannot be rationalised, for here we are concerned with existential life. In these professions which serve human individuality, owing to the isolation of the technical world in conjunction with the increase in specialised ability and the quantity of output, there ensues as a first and concurrent result a simultaneous decline in the practical vocation. True, the mass-order inevitably demands rationalisation in its disposal of the material means. But in the professions of which I am now speaking the vital question is how far this process of rationalisation can go and how far it is self-limited in order to leave scope for the individual to act on his own initiative instead of blindly

66

obeying instructions. Here, joy in work grows out of a harmony between human existence and an activity to which the doers give themselves unreservedly because what they are doing is done for a whole. This joy in work is ruined whenever the working of the universal order is such as to split up the whole into partial functions, those who perform them being indifferently replaceable. When that happens, the ideal of a whole falls into decay. What had previously demanded the staking of the entire being upon the continuity of constructive achievement has now been degraded to become a mere parergon. To-day the resistance of those who strive for the genuine fulfilment of a professional ideal is still dispersed and impotent—and seems, indeed, to be incessantly and inevitably on the decline.

As an example, let me refer to the change that has been taking place in medical practice. In large measure, patients are now dealt with in the mass according to the principles of rationalisation, being sent to institutes for technical treatment, the sick being classified in groups and referred to this or that specialised department. But in this way the patient is deprived of his doctor. The supposition is that, like everything else, medical treatment has now become a sort of manufactured article. An attempt is made to replace personal confidence in a physician by confidence in an institution. But doctor and patient refuse to allow themselves to be placed upon the "conveyor" of organisation. It is true that the service for immediate aid in cases of accident functions, but the vitally central help given by the doctor to the sick man in the continuity of his life is rendered impossible on the "conveyor" method. A gigantic "enterprise" of medical practice is arising, in the form of institutions, bureaucracies, a codified system of material achievement. The inclination to apply a new, a newer, the newest method of treatment to the majority of patients coincides with the organisational will of the masses who have been trained in the school of modern technique—with the will of those who contend (mostly under stress of political emotion) that they can bring healing to all. "Enterprise" has taken the place of individualised care. It would seem that if this path be followed to its logical conclusion, the thoroughly trained and cultured physician, who not only stakes his word as to his personal responsibility but genuinely assumes such responsibility, and who can therefore only deal with a restricted number of patients (for only with a restricted number can a physician establish personal ties)—is likely to die out. Joy in the exercise of a profession on humanist lines, is replaced by the joy in work that results from technical achievement in a field where the cleavage between selfhood and the worker has become established. Such a cleavage, inevitable in other domains of activity likewise, dominates achievement. Unavoidable limitations are imposed upon the absorption of medical activity into the life-order. Public organisation of achievement breaks down when it is misused. A maximal exploitation of the advantages of public services misleads both patients and doctors. There arises a tendency to go on the sick-list in order to enjoy sick benefit; the doctor becomes inclined to treat the largest number of patients at lightning speed, for in this way alone can he gain his livelihood in view of the trifling fees paid for services rendered to panel patients. Thereupon attempts are made to put an end to the abuses of the system by further legislation and control —the result being to restrict yet more the possibilities of such work as can only be done by the true physician. Above all, however, those who are really sick find it less and less possible to have faith that they are being treated thoroughly, scientifically, and intelligently by a doctor whose whole services are for the time put at his service. The human being as a sick man forfeits his rights when there no longer exist any true physicians because the apparatus designed to place them at the disposal of the masses has, by its very working, made the existence of true physicians impossible.

The study of other professions would show in like manner how universally their essence is menaced by modern developments. Fundamentally this destruction of professional joy in work is dependent upon the limits of the life-order, which here can make nothing, but can very easily ruin what is indispensable to itself. Then arises the profound dissatisfaction of the individual robbed of his possibilities; of the doctor and the patient, of the teacher and the taught; and so on. However vigorously they work or overwork, they still lack the consciousness of true fulfilment. More and more do we find that what can only exist as the outcome of individual initiative is being transformed into collective enterprise, in the hope of attaining a vaguely conceived end by collective means, and apparently in the belief that the masses can be satisfied as if they constituted a dominant sort of person. The ideals of the profession fade. Professional persons devote themselves to particular purposes, plans, and organisations. The devastation wrought is at its height where the institutions appear to be in perfect technical order whilst the human beings who work in them lack air to breathe.

Sport. The self-preservative impulse as a form of vitality finds scope for itself in sport; and as a vestige

69

of the satisfaction of immediate life, finds scope for itself in discipline, versatility, adroitness. Through bodily activities subjected to the control of the will, energy and courage are sustained, and the individual seeking contact with nature draws nearer to the elemental forces of the universe.

Sport as a mass-phenomenon, organised on compulsory lines as a game played according to rule, provides an outlet for impulses which would otherwise endanger the apparatus. By occupying their leisure, it keeps the masses quiet. The will to vitality as a movement in air and sunshine is an essentially social manifestation; it has no contemplative relationship to nature as a cipher to be elucidated, and it makes an end of fruitful solitude. The exercise of the combative instinct or of the desire to excel in sport demands the utmost skill, each competitor wishing to establish his superiority over the others. For those animated by this impulse, the all-important thing is to make a record. Publicity and applause are essential. The necessity of observing the rules of the game establishes an obedience to good form, thanks to which in the actual struggle of life rules are likewise observed which facilitate social intercourse.

The venturesome doings of individuals show forth what is unattainable by the masses, but what the masses admire as heroism and feel they would themselves like to do if they could. Such exemplars stake their lives as mountain-climbers, swimmers, aviators, and boxers. These, too, are victims, at the sight of whose achievements the masses are enthused, alarmed, and gratified, being inspired all the while with the secret hope that they themselves, perhaps, may become enabled to do extraordinary things.

A collaborating factor in promoting a delight in

sport may, however, be that which, in classical Rome, unquestionably helped to attract crowds to the gladiatorial shows, namely the pleasure that is felt in witnessing the danger and destruction of persons remote from the spectator's own lot. In like manner the savagery of the crowd is also manifested in a fondness for reading detective stories, a feverish interest in the reports of criminal trials, an inclination towards the absurd and the primitive and the obscure. In the clarity of rational thought, where everything is known or unquestionably knowable, where destiny has ceased to prevail and only chance remains, where (despite all activity) the whole becomes insufferably tedious and absolutely stripped of mystery—there stirs among those who no longer believe themselves to have a destiny establishing ties between themselves and the darkness, the human urge towards the alluring contemplation of eccentric possibilities. The apparatus sees to it that this urge shall be gratified.

Even so, the activities of modern man in sport are not made fully comprehensible through an understanding of what such mass-instincts as the aforesaid can make out of sport. Looming above sport as an organised enterprise wherein the human being forced into the labour mechanism seeks nothing more than an equivalent for his immediate self-preservative impulse, we discern, we feel, in the sport movement, something that is nevertheless great. Sport is not only play and the making of records; it is likewise a soaring and a refreshment. To-day it imposes its demands on every one. Even a life that is over-sophisticated gives itself up to sport under stress of natural impulse. Some, indeed, compare the sport of contemporary human beings with that of classical days. In those times, however, sport was, as it were, an indirect participation of the extraordinary man in his divine origin; and of this there is no longer any thought to-day. But even contemporary human beings wish to express themselves in one way or another, and sport becomes a philosophy. They rise in revolt against being cabined, cribbed, confined; and they seek relief in sport, though it lacks transcendental substantiality. Still, it contains the aforesaid soaring element—unconsciously willed, though without communal content—as a defiance to the petrified present. The human body is demanding its own rights in an epoch when the apparatus is pitilessly annihilating one human being after another. Modern sport, therefore, is enveloped in an aura which, though the respective historical origins differ, makes it in some ways akin to the sport of the antique world. Contemporary man, when engaged in sport, does not indeed become a Hellene, but at the same time he is not a mere fanatic of sport. We see him when he is engaged in sport as a man who, strapped in the straitwaistcoat of life, in continuous peril as if engaged in active warfare, is nevertheless not crushed by his almost intolerable lot, but strikes a blow in his own behalf, stands erect to cast his spear.

But even though sport imposes one of the limits upon the rationalised life-order, through sport alone man cannot win to freedom. Not merely by keeping his body fit, by soaring upward in vital courage, and by being careful to "play the game", can he overcome the danger of losing his self.

4. IMPOSSIBILITY OF A STEADFAST LIFE-ORDER

If life could be satisfactorily arranged, one would have to presuppose the possibility of a steadfast lifeorder. It is obvious, however, that no such stable condition is possible. Life, being essentially imperfect, and, as we know it, intolerable, is continually seeking to re-fashion the life-order under new forms.

Not even the technical apparatus can attain finality. We might conceive of the using-up of our planet as the locale and substance of a gigantic factory, run by the masses of mankind. In the planet as thus conceived, there would no longer persist anything purely and directly natural. The material out of which the apparatus was made would, of course, be a gift of nature, but, having been applied to human purposes, would have been used up and would no longer have an independent being. The only substance remaining in the world would be that which had already been moulded by man. The world itself would be like an artificial landscape, consisting exclusively of this man-made apparatus in space and time, a unique product each of whose parts would be kept in touch with one another by incessantly-working means of communication, human beings being fettered to the apparatus in order, by their joint labour, to continue to make for themselves the necessaries of life. Thus a stable condition would have been achieved. We may suppose that all the matter and all the energy in the world would be continually utilised without reserve. Population would be regulated by birth control. The sciences of eugenics and hygiene would see to it that the best possible human beings were being bred. Diseases would have been abolished. There would be a purposive economy wherein, by compulsory social service, the needs of all would be supplied. No further decisions would have to be made. In the cycle of the recurring generations, everything would go on unchanged. Without struggle and without the spice of hazard, the joys of life would be provided for all in unalterable allotments, with the expenditure of little labour and with ample scope for pastime.

In truth, however, such a condition of affairs is impossible. It is prevented by the working of incalculable natural forces, whose devastating effects can become intensified to technical catastrophes. There may also be the specific misfortune of a failure of technique. Perhaps the persistence of the scientific campaign against diseases, temporarily to all appearance overwhelming in its success, will rob human beings of their immunity, will deprive them of it so completely that an unanticipated pestilence will sweep away the whole race. The notion that people will generally and for an indefinite period remain content to practise birth control has been too readily adopted; the struggles that have to be faced by an indefinitely-increasing population will be renewed through the working of the will to reproduction, which is stronger in some members of our species than in others. Eugenics will prove unable to hinder the survival of the weakly, and will fail to prevent that racial deterioration which would seem unavoidable amid the conditions of modern civilisation—for we have no objective standard of values to guide us in eugenic selection, and the idea of such a standard becomes almost unthinkable in view of the multiplicity of the primitive stocks out of which the human species has sprung.

Nor can we conceive of any permanent condition which would bring content. Technical advances do not create a perfected world, but at every stage introduce fresh difficulties and therewith new tasks into an imperfect world. Not merely does improved technique bring about an increasing discontent with its lack of perfection, but it has to remain imperfect under pain of collapse. Whatever frontiers technique may have momentarily reached, it cannot continue to subsist without the spirit of discovery, invention, planning, and new creation; and these will force it to overstep the aforesaid frontiers.

We learn from a study of the whole that mankind can never definitively attain a thoroughly purposive life-order, inasmuch as this order itself is rent in sunder by internal oppositions. The result of this internecine struggle is that the life-order moves restlessly onward through the ages in inevitable imperfection. Not merely do we find that, concretely, State wars against State, party against party, the sense of the State against economic interests, class against class, and one economic interest against another—but that the very forces which bring our life into being are themselves full of antinomies. Self-interest as the working motor of individual activity fashions, at one time, vital conditions which promote the general interest, and, at another time, destroys these same conditions. The orderly machinery, with its sharply delimitated functions, duties, and rights of atomised human beings all regarded as perfectly interchangeable, arms itself against initiative, against individual venturesomeness, which threatens orderliness—and yet this machinery itself could not, in the absence of such initiative, continue to adapt itself to the perpetually changing situations of its environment.

Unless organisation be held in check by contraposing forces, it will ruin what it would fain safeguard, man as man. A bee community is possible as a static structure, perpetually reproducible; but human life, whether for the individual or for the community at large, is only possible as historical destiny, only as the incalculable course of technical achievements, economic enterprise, political ordinances.

Man can live only when, using his reason and working in co-operation with his fellows, he busies himself about the ordering of the technical supply of mass-needs. He must, therefore, devote himself with ardour to the cares of this world unless he is himself to perish amid its decay. He brings a world of purposive order into existence by striving to transcend its limitations wherever they show themselves. The limits of the life-order are in this matter his adversaries; and yet, in such limitations, he himself, since he is not absorbed into the order, is likewise personally present. Were he to become unreservedly master of the adversaries of the life-order, he would be hopelessly merged in the world of his own creation. Man's situation does not become a truly mental one until he grows aware of himself in these limitary positions. There he is truly living as himself when life, instead of rounding itself off, forces upon him continually-renewed antinomies.

5. ATTEMPTS TO JUSTIFY THE ESTABLISHING OF A LIFE-ORDER THAT SHALL HAVE BEEN RENDERED ABSOLUTE (MODERN SOPHISTRY)

The realisation of the existence of economic forces, of masses, of apparatus, of mechanisation, has, through research, led to the growth of a science which claims universal validity. In actual fact the reality embodied in it is a mighty one. It has become a new, and at length a spiritual force. Nevertheless, insofar as it claims to be anything more than the rational control of purposive activity, insofar as it puts forward a claim to absolute status as a picture of life in its entirety, it has become, so to say, a creed or a faith which the spirit must either accept or resist. Whilst scientific research in particular (as far as this field is concerned)

76

is occupied in the study of the qualities and quantities of economic forces, what is decisive in our consciousness of the mental situation is the answer we give to the question whether these economic forces and their results are the only and the universally dominant realities for mankind.

The claim that an all-embracing life-order shall have an absolute validity is based in some such fashion as the following. Life is to be regarded as the purposive satisfaction of the elementary vital needs of all. The human mind enters into this world, claiming it for its own. Joy in work must not be in any way diminished, but must, rather, promote the satisfaction of needs, and must contribute to the improvement of working methods, technique, and sociological apparatus. The individual's life must be entirely devoted to the service of the whole, thanks to which he simultaneously achieves the partial gratification of his own self-seeking (within the limits of the possible). Thus there arises the closed circuit of self-preserving human life, an orbit wherein life must revolve for ever—for it is utopian to imagine that joy in the general life will become identical with joy in the work which makes life possible for all. Judged by the standard of the greatest happiness of the greatest number, the meaning of human life is the economic provision of the largest possible mass of people with the amplest opportunities for gratifying their manifold needs.

All the same, the trend of this realisation cannot be pursued to its logical end, and, furthermore, the dominance of such images in the modern consciousness is by no means an absolute one. Technique, apparatus, and mass-life are far from exhausting the being of man. It is true that the titanic tools and forms of this life-world, the instruments of his own making, react upon him; but they do not wholly or unreservedly control his being. They influence him, but he remains different from them. Man cannot be deduced from a restricted number of principles. The construction of such principles, while throwing light upon certain relationships, makes it all the plainer that there is much which lies altogether outside of them.

Consequently, with the science of this life-order (insofar as it is regarded as having an absolute validity), there is unwittingly associated, either an erroneous belief in the possibility of attaining a definitively stable and sound world-organisation, or else an utter hopelessness in respect of all human life. Those who look forward to a routinist satisfaction with the welfare of the whole, to such a degree of welfare as might conceivably be attainable, tacitly ignore undesirable but undeniable facts. But instead of swinging like a pendulum between affirmation and denial of life as thus contemplated, we should continually strive to keep ourselves aware of the limits of the life-order. When we do this, the notion that the life-order can be rendered absolute becomes impossible for us to entertain; and our consciousness, relieved of its burden, recognising a reality that is knowable in its relativity, is free to turn to another possibility.

But if the notion that the life-order for the supply of mass-needs can have an absolute validity be allowed to persist, this inevitably leads to a mental attitude (that of the modern sophists) which manifests the unfathomability of the mind in respect of a reality thus rendered absolute.

Idolisation of the Masses. To the question, "What is the true upshot?" those who want to establish an absolute wherein the goal is clearly cognised by the understanding can give no answer. Still, in the urgent desire to find a justification, the general interest, the whole, the reason, and mass-life (as the real life of human beings), are bandied about as catchwords wherewith—since as thus used they have a perpetually fluctuating significance—anything or everything can be established or refuted.

The manifold significance of the concept of the mass is, in very truth, an extremely definite one, and one which is utterly opposed to the establishing of an absolute. Nevertheless, any reference to the masses to-day arouses uncontrollable excitement. The implication would seem to be that the mass-idea, though clearly definable, is to become tantamount to the entire content of human history and to purposiveness. The word "masses" befools us, that we may be misled into thinking of mankind under the category of multiplicity as if it were a single nameless unity. But the masses cannot, in any definable sense, become the bearers of that essence which makes man what he is. Every individual, inasmuch as he is a possible existence, is something more than a mere member of the masses, makes untransferable claims upon himself, and must not be merged in the masses in such a way as to forfeit his right to independent existence as a human being. An appeal to the idea of the masses is a sophistical instrument for the maintenance of vain enterprises, for fleeing from oneself, for evading responsibility, and for renouncing the attempt to climb towards true humanhood.

The Language of Mystification and Revolt. The limits of the rational life-order become visible in the impossibility of understanding and justifying this life intrinsically. To maintain the fiction that it has an absolute validity, its exponents have to employ a language of mystification. The methodical use of such mystification is more prevalent in proportion as it becomes impossible to achieve a rational justification. Its standard is the "utmost welfare of the community" assumed to be calculable; its interest is the satisfaction of all those who are to fulfil their functions in a quiet and orderly manner. It always has compensating instances ready to be adduced as a set-off against the horrors of life. What has really to be effected by the use of compulsion has the compulsion veiled by ascribing responsibility for it to some impalpable authority. The apparatus can venture to use force in a way which no individual would dare. In case of a deadlock, an appeal is made to science, which is ready to appear in court as the expert, thus playing the part of handmaid to the public interest conceived as identical with the life-order. In extreme cases this is a quite illegitimate appeal. When an expert neither knows nor can know the facts, he has to help himself out with formulas which provide a semblance of knowledge for the justification of political acts by legal interpretations, for the justification of certain para-graphs in the criminal code (those, for instance, relating to abortion, capital punishment, etc.), for the explanation of neuroses following on accidents, in such a way as will diminish the pecuniary responsibility of the apparatus as employer, and so on. In the last resort what is actually said appears to be a matter of indifference, the formula's standard of value being a determination to maintain order and to mask anything which would put order to the question.

On the other side we have the language of revolt. It belongs to the mass-order just as much as does the language of mystification and appeasement, but adopts a different method of confusing the issues. Instead of directing its gaze thoughtfully towards a whole, it tries to bring the individual into the limelight. In the glare, each individual is blind to the others. A medley ensues in which the revolutionists appeal to all sorts of obscure impulses, justifying them with the one aim of justifying disturbance and revolt. Just as the language of rational justification with its appeal to the general welfare becomes a vehicle of order, so does the language of isolating revolt become a vehicle of destruction.

Life totters, not really understanding the speech it is itself using. The uncertainty of its purposes and its will becomes plain in those cases where the matter in question has really nothing to do with the technical provision of the elementary necessaries of human life, but is falsely presented as being thus concerned. At such times those who give themselves out to be reasonable and practical are, in reality, utterly per-plexed. When nothing that convinces can be added to the discussion, recourse is had to some colourful emotional phrase introduced for the express pur-pose of prejudging the case. From the mouths of those who have lost their way in life, there frequently come such expressions as "the sanctity of life", "the majesty of death", "the majesty of the people", "the will of the people is the will of God", "service of the people", etc. While thus evading discussion, they indirectly disclose that they are speaking of things which do not form a part of any life-order; and since they have cut loose from their own roots they cannot really know what they want. This sophistry vacil-litates between the opportunist adroitness of selfish life, on the one hand, and an irrational emotional drive, on the other.

When there is a demand that a great multitude of persons should do something, although no one has any clear idea of what has to be done and why, so that no one knows whither to direct his will, there result the mystifications of impotence. Those who occupy leading positions, appeal to unity, or to responsibility, and demand sobriety of thought. It is necessary, they say, to reckon with extant facts, and to be practical rather than theoretical; anything likely to arouse irritation must be avoided, but at the same time the attacks must be warded off by all permissible means; the main thing, however, is to leave the guidance of affairs to the established leaders, who will know what it is best to do in the particular concatenation of circumstances. But such leaders as these, who use brave words while in their secret hearts they do not know what they want, are persons who will stay where they are and let matters drift, watching idly, and not daring to come to any decision.

Irresolution. The life-order has a pre-eminent need of tranquillity as its safeguard, and its champions sophistically represent their dread of coming to a decision as the best way of promoting the general interest.

The insatiability of desire is restrained in individuals, in groups, in organisations, and in parties, by all agreeing to resist one another's encroachments. That is why compromise so often masquerades as justice. But compromise is either an artificial binding together of heterogeneous interests to form the specious unity of a life-institution, or else it is nothing more than a reciprocal yielding of points in order to avoid having to come to a decision. It is true that in community life any one who encounters an opposing activity is constrained to desire understanding and not struggle, if he desires this community life to continue. He therefore, within limits, renounces self-seeking, that he may render the continuance of life possible in the long run. He distinguishes his selfhood, which is unconditioned, from life, which is relative, and thus, as selfhood, has the power for compromise. But the question necessarily arises, what is the boundary between the compromise whose presupposition is the energy of deciding selfhood, and the compromise which leads to the dissolution of selfhood by becoming no more than the extremity of levelling co-operation on the part of all.

For when, in any matter, a man is wholly himself, he recognises that there are alternatives, and then his action will not be a compromise. He will want to force a decision between the alternatives he has recognised. He knows that he may come to wreck, is well acquainted with primitive resignation as regards the duration of life, and is aware that a sincere failure may but emphasise the reality of his being. But for one who is exclusively animated by self-seeking impulses, so that in the life-order he makes partial renunciation merely in order to safeguard himself in the whole, the struggle brings risks which he cannot face. He only uses force when the big battalions are on his side, and shuns decision which involves danger. As long as his present life remains possible under tolerable conditions, he will accept whatever comes, and will always favour those of moderate views as against the extremists. He abjures anything that seems to him highflown, demanding adaptableness and a peaceful disposition. A frictionless functioning of the enterprise remains the ideal of such persons. They are willing to merge themselves in the co-operative body, pretending that therein each member is supplemented and enlarged by all the others. Not the individual takes precedence, but the general interest, which (when it happens to be definite) is in truth simultaneously particular, and as a "general" interest remains void. The suppression of competition by the formation of cartels is trimmed with frills called the "general interest". Jealousy is neutralised by reciprocally tolerant changes of occupation, and an endeavour is made to mitigate the severity of the struggle for truth by a synthesis of every possibility. Justice becomes unsubstantial, imprecise, as if every one could be ranged upon the same plane as all others. To strive for a decision no longer means to come to grips with fate but to act forcibly in a strongly authoritative position.

But when, thereupon, a revolt occurs, it likewise, owing to the sophistical perversion of opinion and behaviour, leads to no decision, resulting only in a ruinous turning of things topsy-turvy, which, if not controlled by the life-order, must inevitably lead to chaos.

The Mind as a Means. Insofar as everything has been made dependent upon the rendering of the life-order absolute; insofar as the economic forces and situations, the possible powers, strive towards this end—so likewise is mental activity similarly directed, as if this were the one thing that mattered. The mind has ceased to believe in itself, as self-arising, and becomes a means to an end. Having thus grown fully mobile as a mere instrument of sophistry, it can serve any master. It discovers justification for any state of affairs, either extant or regarded as desirable by the powers that be. Yet the mind knows, all the time, that its working cannot be seriously regarded so long as it works on these lines, and it marks its secret knowledge of itself by the emotionalism of an assumed conviction. Since the awareness of the real powers of life does not only demand this insincerity, but also refuses to allow a veil to be drawn over the essential dependence of all life, there does, indeed, arise a new straightforwardness in the knowledge of the inevitable. All the same, forthwith the demand for a sober sense of reality becomes the sophistical instrument of everything which is not perfectly obvious, and man's true will is thereby ruined. This insincerity in its incredible manifoldedness cannot fail to result from the perversion of human possibilities if life continue to be regarded as the order or system for supplying the masses with the general necessaries of life.

6. CRITICAL CONDITION OF THE PRESENT LIFE-ORDER

Imminent seems the collapse of that which for millenniums has constituted man's universe. The new world which has arisen as an apparatus for the supply of the necessaries of life compels everything and every one to serve it. It annihilates whatever it has no place for. Man seems to be undergoing absorption into that which is nothing more than a means to an end, into that which is devoid of purpose or significance. But therein he can find no satisfaction. It does not provide him with the things which give him value and dignity. That which, amid the needs and stresses of the past, had persisted as an unquestioned background of his being, is now in course of disappearance. While he is expanding his life, he would seem to be sacrificing the being in which he realises his own selfhood.

Very general, therefore, is the conviction that there is something amiss with the scheme of things, that what really matters is out of order. Everything has become questionable; the substance of everything is threatened. It used to be said that we were living in a time of transition, but now every newspaper is talking of the world-crisis.

People who look for deeper causes discover the critical condition of the State, saying that when the method of government does not lead to the formation of any decisive will towards the whole, and that when the mood of assent vacillitates, all foundations begin to crumble. Others speak of a crisis in civilisation, resulting from the decomposition of our spiritual life. Yet others, finally, declare that the crisis affects the entire being of mankind. The limits of a mass-order that claims to be absolute are becoming so plainly disclosed that the world staggers.

The crisis realises itself as a lack of confidence. If people still cling to the coercion of the law, if they are still convinced by power, and by the rigidity of convention, it is only because of a calculus of material advantages, and not from any real confidence. When all has been reduced to the purposiveness of life-interests, the consciousness of the substantiality of the whole has been destroyed.

To-day, in actual fact, no cause, no office, no profession, no person, is regarded as worthy of trust until, in each concrete instance, satisfactory grounds for confidence have been disclosed. Every well-informed person is acquainted with the deceptions, the deviations, the untrustworthiness that prevail in his own familiar domain. Where confidence persists, it is only within very narrow circles, for it never extends to the totality. The crisis is universal, all-embracing. It is of multiple causation, so that it cannot be overcome by dealing with this or that particular cause, but must be apprehended, endured, and mastered as our world-wide destiny.

From the outlook of technique and economics, all the problems mankind has to solve would seem to have become planetary in their scope. It is not merely that on the surface of our globe there has ensued a general interlacement of the economic conditions upon which the technical mastery of life depends, so that the world can only nowadays work as a unit; for an increasing number of persons have come to look upon it as demanding unification into a circumscribed area on which alone, under such unified conditions, their history can work itself out. The Great War was the first war in which practically the whole of mankind was involved.

With the unification of our planet there has begun a process of levelling-down which people contemplate with horror. That which has to-day become general to our species is always the most superficial, the most trivial, and the most indifferent of human possibilities. Yet men strive to effect this levelling-down as if, in that way, the unification of mankind could be brought about. On tropical plantations and in the fishing villages of the Far North, the films of the great capitals are thrown on the screen. People dress alike. The conventionalities of daily intercourse are cosmopolitan; the same dances, the same types of thought, and the same catchwords (a compost derived from the Enlightenment, from Anglo-Saxon positivism, and from theological tradition) are making their way all over the world. At world congresses the same levelling-down is furthered by those who, instead of aspiring to promote communication between heterogeneous entities, want unification upon a common basis in religion and philosophy. The races of man interbreed. The historical civilisations and cultures become detached from their roots, and are merged in the technico-economic world and in a vacant intellectualism.

Of course this process is as yet only in its beginnings, but every one, children no less than grown-ups, is subject to its influence. The first intoxication of an expanding world is giving place to a sense of restriction. It actually surprises us to learn that when a zeppelin crosses Siberia, people should hide from it in alarm. Those who remain permanently settled in the place where they were born seem to have stuck in the mud.

One of the most notable characteristics of our day is a progressive and irremediable loss of substance. For a century there has been a continuous decline in the level of the physiognomical expression of the generations. From every profession there arise complaints of the lack of effective individualities despite a continuous inrush of new aspirants. On all hands we see a swarm of mediocrities, interspersed among whom are the specifically gifted functionaries of the apparatus, who concentrate it and find in it careers. The persistence of almost all the expressional possibilities of the past results in a wellnigh impenetrable confusion. The upshot is parade instead of true being, multiplicity instead of unity, garrulousness instead of the imparting of real knowledge, experience instead of existence—interminable mimicry.

There is a mental or spiritual cause for this decay. Authority used to be the form of interconnexion through mutual confidence, giving law to uncertainties, and linking the individual with the consciousness of being. During the nineteenth century, this form was definitively fused and destroyed in the fires of criticism. The result, on the one hand, has been the cynicism characteristic of modern life. People shrug their shoulders when contemplating the vulgarities and trivialities that are rife in great matters no less than in small. On the other hand, strict attention to duty, self-sacrificing loyalty, have disappeared. With a pliable humaneness from which *humanitas* has vanished, and with an anæmic idealism, we justify the most pitiful and most casual of happenings. Now that we have become disenchanted with science, we recognise that the world has grown godless, and that no unqualified law of freedom any longer prevails. Instead, there is nothing but order, participation, non-interference. No exercise of our will can re-establish genuine authority, for the attempt to do this would but lead to the setting up of a regime of unyielding force. Only from new beginnings can anything effective come. Criticism is certainly the pre-condition of a change for the better, but it is not in itself creative. Although formerly criticism was a life-producing power, it is now dispersed and decayed, turning against itself, and leading to the instability caused by doing whatever one likes. Its significance can no longer be to judge and to guide in accordance with valid rules, for its true task is to appreciate facts and to say what really exists. But it cannot do this unless it be reanimated by a genuine content and by the possibility of a self-creative world.

To the question, "What still exists to-day?" we answer: "A consciousness of peril and loss as a consciousness of the radical crisis." At present, existence is a mere possibility, not something possessed and guaranteed. All objectivity has become ambiguous: the true seems irrevocably lost; substance, perplexity: reality, a masquerade. He who wishes to find his way to the origin of the crisis must pass through the lost domain of truth, in order to revise it possessively;

must traverse the domain of perplexity to reach decision concerning himself; must strip off the trappings of the masquerade, in order to disclose the genuine that lies beneath.

A new world cannot arise out of the crisis through the work of the rational life-order as such. What is needful is that the human being shall achieve something more than he brings to pass in the life-order, shall achieve it by way of the State as expressive of the will towards the whole, by the State to which the life-order has become nothing but a means—and also through mental creation, whereby he grows aware of his own being. Along both these roads he can regain consciousness of the origin and the aim of human existence in the nobility of free self-creation, cognisance of which has been lost in the life-order. If he fancies that he has found the most essential of his requirements in the State, then experience teaches him that the State in and by itself falls short of his hopes, and merely offers scope for the realisation of possibilities. If he confides in the mind, as a being in and by itself, he finds that this is questionable in every one of its extant objectivisations. He has to go back to the very beginning, to human existence, out of which the State and the mind derive blood and reality.

Therewith he renders relative the only tie which can be all-embracing, namely purposive thought, reasonable thought, applied to the objective order of the world. But the truth which produces community in being is a temporary historical faith which can never be the faith of all. No doubt the truth of reasonable insight is the same for all, but the truth which man himself is and which induces clarity in his faith, severs him. In the unending struggle of primitive communication, the alien flares up, dissent is bred, and for this reason man becoming aware of himself in the contemporary mental situation rejects any faith or belief that is authoritatively imposed from without. What remains comprehensible as the unity of the whole is the historical aspect of this state, mind as a life linked with its origin, man in his for-the-time-being specific and irreplaceable essence.

PART TWO

WILL IN THE WHOLE

THE unavoidability of the life-order finds its limit in the human being who refuses to be wholly absorbed into a function; and further in this, that no unique and perfected and definitive life-order is possible. The human being who wants to be something more than mere life, decides what shall be chosen and what shall be safeguarded; in default of this he accepts life as it is and allows everything to be decided for him.

The decision which the human being as an individual achieves, internally, in respect of his own being, is, in fact, the inviolable authority of that being. But reality can only exist in a world through the wisdom of the power in the whole wherein human beings can attain to a unity of will in respect of the organisation of their condition and their self-maintenance in the world. What man really becomes depends upon the will of this power, which decides the historical concreteness of life in the whole. That power is at any time politically incorporated in the State; and, as the tradition of historical human existence, it is education.

Insofar as conscious will has anything to do with the matter, our future entirely depends upon political and educational activity. A tensing of the will to act upon things despite a sense of impotence as regards their course is the courage of selfhood in politically acting human beings; and the force of the educator is that which makes him strive his utmost, in defiance of a sense of impotence as regards the influencing of human conduct, to make man attain the highest possibilities through the utilisation of the profoundest content of what has been handed down to him.

The whole, however, is never the whole without qualification. Wherever man presses onward to discover the supreme authority in the world, at the point of decisive origin he encounters something which transcends both State and education.

1. THE STATE

As soon as the reality of the whole as the place of ultimate decision has been consciously realised, the will to the State or the sense of the State is the grip on the lever by which from time to time decisions are made. The will to the State or the sense of the State is the will of man to shape his own destiny, which never exists for him purely as an individual, but only in a community formed by the succession of generations. The will of the State, however, has to express itself amid a multiplicity of competing States, and is subject to internal tensions resulting from the endeavour to give the State its definite historical form.

For the State-will, the life-order is not merely the object of rational planning on behalf of all human beings, for it becomes the object of exclusive decisions through encroachment upon its powers. The State-will does indeed incorporate the idea of promoting the general welfare by means of the economic life-order, but, over and above this, it is directed towards man himself.

Since the State-will cannot bring this about by purposive voluntary action, it must be content to create the requisite possibilities upon the ideal plane. The State-will must seek its path amid insoluble tensions; its peculiar position in the world (as a world-historical situation) compels it to increase its power at the expense of the development of its intrinsic humanity. Conversely, human existence constrains it to restrict the development of its powers, for otherwise its fundamental purpose, the highest possible development of man, would be frustrated. Although for the time being and for a brief space in the statesman and in the soldier this tension may pass into abeyance and may culminate in the elevation of some particular human being who, by this very elevation, becomes the power of his State—still, in the long run, there is no means of avoiding the persistence of the tension between the necessities of the momentary situation, on the one hand, and, on the other, the essential goal, which is to promote the higher development of mankind. Consequently the State-will may grasp at a temporary and specious success; but it can also, under spell of a spiritual ideal, outsoar the realities of the moment in favour of an imaginary future and thus cheat itself of life.

The concrete content of the State is the providing of man with opportunities for the free fulfilment of his occupational ideals in all their multiplicity—ideals which cannot be fulfilled so long as he remains a mere function in the apparatus; and the substance upon which the State works consists of human beings who, through education, have acquired the power of participating in their historical tradition. In both respects, the State, while safeguarding the mass-order because this can only continue to exist in virtue of the State, can at the same time provide safeguards against the mass-order.

Sense of the State. With the arising of a sense of the State, man became aware of that authoritative force which, in our own days, continually decides the existence and the movement of things. The State claimed a monopoly of the legitimate use of force (Max Weber).

Therewith two results ensued. First of all, the use of force was excluded from the ordering of everyday life, which thenceforward could be carried on peacefully in accordance with rules and laws. In the second place, force was intensified in the only region where it becomes perfectly clear that without force, actual or potential, human life cannot persist. The application of force, previously dispersed, has been concentrated. Whereas the individual human being had of old to be continually prepared to protect and to expand his life by the personal use of weapons, he has now become the instrument for the technical application of force which has been canalised by the State. Only a small proportion of the population is occupationally enrolled in the police force, but in case of war every male fit to bear arms becomes part of the armed power of the State. Thus the State incorporates power which either implies a tacit threat of force or decides matters by the actual use of force. As the situation varies, the use of force may be intensified to a maximum or reduced to a minimum.

For the individual, the mental situation would be the demand that he should adapt himself to the reality of power, since he only exists in virtue of the existence of that power, and, in a sense, it is also his own power. For the State would not be the State if it were nothing more than a blind exercise of force; it becomes the State only through the successful working of mental acts which, in their freedom, know themselves linked with reality as it exists here and now. The State may decline into the chaos of crude force, or it may aspire and rise as the ideal of that which promotes the wisdom of human existence and also of the will which grasps power. The State, therefore, may either lose its way in a realm of crude and vain force, which calls in sophistry to its service, and which I shall then regard as I regard nature (which can and will annihilate me, but which, insofar as I can do nothing against it, is really no concern of mine); or, on the other hand, it may be a historically interlinked substantial power, if an obscure demand of reality becomes clarified in the mentally conscious will. To-day the mental reality of the State seems decaying, but has not utterly vanished away.

When the State was supposed to incorporate the authority of a will legitimised by the Deity, the broad masses of human beings subjected themselves to the few who ruled, and accepted as the dispensations of Providence all that was decreed from above. But when, as to-day, there is a general awareness that State action as such is not the expression of a divine will which it is incumbent upon men to obey, there has become dominant a conception of the State as an expression of the human will, of a general will in which each individual will participates. Man lives in the mass-order between the poles of the peaceful apparatus for providing the necessaries of life, on the one hand, and, on the other, the powers actually perceptible from moment to moment, the powers whose direction and content he wants to know so that he can exert an influence upon them.

Man can no longer mask the actualities of power by regarding them as nothing more than the vestiges of reputed terrors of the past, presumed to be capable of being abolished once and for all. To those who look facts honestly in the face it is clear that every order only exists through power, for the reason that it impinges upon the limits of a will alien to it. Whether the power of the State be looked upon as something requisite for making head against this alien power, or whether the power itself be regarded as evil because the State puts forward the claim to monopolise the use of force, we reach here the obscure foundations of community life where all activity (if power be in itself evil) is a matter of coming to terms with the non-rational and the anti-human. It may happen that upon these obscure foundations the resolute will builds the continuity of historical possibility; or it may happen that irresolute activities pursue the satisfaction of dispersed and temporary interests, using force only to promote these. Our social existence persists in time through being moulded by this power.

The State, in itself neither legitimate nor illegitimate, is not deducible from anything else, but is the self-establishing life of the will to which power has been allotted and which has assumed power for itself. The result is a perpetual struggle in behalf of the State, and a struggle between States. For the State is never the exclusive power of all mankind upon earth, but is always one power beside others, sometimes allied with them and sometimes in conflict with them. Always, indeed, there is an endeavour to establish a legal order, but every existing legal order is somewhere and somehow based upon force, sustained by struggle and warfare, which decide under what forms of dependence and in virtue of what principles the legal order shall exist. There is no definitive repose. Situations vary; the forces thanks to whose concentration power comes into being, diminish or increase. Instead of achieving the establishment of a world-State, all that results is that mankind at large passes into a condition of unrest through identification with its own historical situation.

There is no sense in idolising the State nor yet in painting it blacker than we need. Emotional eloquence blinds contending parties to the truth, to reality, instead of making them aware how life is determined. The main difference· between men is, whether they are inwardly convinced of the historical transformation of life as our destiny, or blandly accept the repose of an illusionary world of human brotherliness or of dissatisfaction, remaining inert amid the pleasures and pains of life—until unanticipated destruction manifests the futility of their deception.

Now that the charm has been dispelled which first brought the State into the light-pencil of questioning and of the desire for knowledge, the contemporary mental situation enables every one to enter this region of human community life. To every one the dreadfulness of the world of human activity in the domain of State reality will appear in its full inexorability. But he who is not paralysed with terror by the vision, he who does not forget and does not turn his eyes away from reality, will press onward to the point of a participating knowledge in this reality of human action and human self-determination—to the point at which it will become clear to him what he really wants, not in general and universally, but historically and in conjunction with those of his fellows who appear to him truly human.

To be able to think politically denotes the attainment of so high a level in the human scale that we can scarcely expect every one to reach such a level. There are two opposing possibilities, two opposing ways along which man may renounce his political possibilities.

He may decide to refrain from participation in the course of events. No doubt he will remain interested in the advantages he can procure from the chances of his own life. But for him the whole is nothing more than the affairs of others, whose concern, whose profession, it is to see to these things. No doubt we are constantly brought up with a jar against the effects of force as used in the existing order. We find this or that unjust or unmeaning. But those who have adopted the evasion of responsibility I am now considering, look upon it as something foreign to themselves, something which is no business of theirs. If they are consistent, they do not complain. Indifferent to the course of events, they do not allow their feelings to become involved. Since they have no guiding lines, either as regards possibilities in general or as concerns the contemporary situation, they honestly acknowledge the fact, and abstain from criticism just as they abstain from action. Their "unpolitical" behaviour is the renouncement effected by those who do not want to know what they will, because they have no will but that of realising themselves in an unworldly selfhood—as if they existed apart from time and space. They accept the historical destiny of man with passive toleration because they have faith in the salvation of the soul—which has no historical validity. Such a man lacks the sense of responsibility of him who, above all, is himself in the world, and who regards himself as guilty of any evil that befalls, insofar as he has failed to do everything in his power to determine what shall happen.

The alternative method of renouncing a true political life is to surrender to a blind political will. One who does this is discontented with his life, and complains of environing circumstances, regarding them, instead of himself, as the cause of the happenings of his life. He is inspired, now with hatred, now with enthusiasm, but above all with the instinct of the will to power. Although he does not know what he might know if he would, and does not know what he really wills, he talks, he chooses, and he acts as though he knew. By a short-circuit he passes abruptly from a quarter-knowledge to the licence of fanaticism. Such vociferous would-be participation is the most widespread manifestation of a reputed political knowledge and will. Persons of this kidney stumble along through the times, able to make trouble and to stir up strife, but utterly incapable of discovering the true path.

To-day it behoves those who do not wish to shirk, to take their part in the life of the State, although this lacks the sanction of an authority which would be derivable from a transcendental justification for its activities, and cannot, on the other hand, be regarded or consolidated as a rationalisable centre for the purposive satisfaction of all human needs. One who deliberately does his best to establish the foundations of the State upon which all human life depends, even though he knows that the State lacks the aforesaid sanctions, is endowed with a true sense of the State. He who inwardly recognises that it is incumbent upon him to do what he can in this field is brought face to face with the problem of human existence. Here he reaches a sphere outside the delusions of those who dream of a harmonious life attainable through the proper organisation of the world. He comes to recognise that he has no right to fancy there can be a definitive knowledge of the nature of the State, nor yet of the huge creature that manifests itself in the form of legality. In the invisible interweaving of human activities and the human will, the individual, in his situation, is delivered over to the historical process which discloses itself in the exercise of political power without being surveyable as a whole. In that region of human affairs, blind will, passionate indignation, impatient desire for possession, become unmeaning. Nothing can be effective but patience, foresight, a restrained and resolute preparedness for studied intervention, comprehensive knowledge, and awareness of the fact that beyond coercive immediate reality the infinite realm of the possible still remains open: anything more than this is mere tumult, destructiveness, unmeaning and petulant activity. In his impotence, however, it is harder for the individual to apprehend his freedom to act, and to realise it, when, as to-day, the reason for it is regarded as purely secular; it is harder to be actuated by a simple sense of mundane responsibility in matters which, heretofore, were left to the divine authority of the State. An endeavour, which can only expect frustration, is made along finite paths to discover a road whose goal is unknown. And yet that goal is the place which, in contradistinction to the methods of a rationalised supply of the necessaries of life, will be disclosed to him alone who, despite everything, can pursue a transcendental aim.

It is easy to understand, therefore, why almost all of us renounce the attempt. Bolshevism and fascism present themselves as easier possibilities. Let us learn once more to obey without question; let us content ourselves with a list of easy catchwords; let us, meanwhile, leave action to some all-powerful individual who has seized the reins of government! These forms of dictatorship are substitutes for true authority, achieved at the cost of renouncing, on the part of almost all of us, the right to be ourselves. In the situation of the contemporary world, the States in which the aforesaid possibilities of evasion have not yet been adopted contemplate them as the realities of other States with which they have to reckon; and in the internal life of the former States, the possibilities in question menace them as demands of the masses.

Selfhood, however, begins with perplexity in face of the real and the possible. The personal life vibrates in sympathy with the contemporaneous world processes, and unceasingly clarifies its knowledge of the possible, until it becomes ripe to collaborate in the shaping of the situation.

In this there will persist the tension between the mass-order for the supply of the necessaries of life, on the one hand, and the decision that is based upon power, on the other; or, in other words, the tension between society and the State.

Man serves the meaning of the life-order for society through work, that work which establishes his own life in society. All rational planning is directed towards an improvement of this order and its functions, towards the prevention of disturbances, towards justice, law, and peace. The social sense of the State is the urge towards such activities.

But unavoidable limits exist: in the qualities of the masses, in the irremediable pitilessness of social and biological selection; in the inequitable restrictions imposed upon the scope of life for the great majority; in the differences between races, characters, and talents; in the varying rate at which population increases in the associated groups. The State, therefore, is to be regarded, not only as the function of safeguarding the legal order of things, but also as the focus of the struggle concerning the kind and the trend of the unavoidable use of force. At all times man has had to suffer torments and to carry heavy burdens. To-day he would gladly, and in full consciousness of what he is doing, liberate himself from these by the best possible organisation of the whole. Since this remains unfulfilled, the social sense of the State is overpowered or overlaid by the political consciousness of destiny.

Only on the abstract plane, therefore, is the mental situation of the State and society one that is general to the time. In reality it is but the situation in a historically particular State, from which the gaze turns towards other States. The laxity of the human individual can, indeed, go so far that he may change his nationality or may become Stateless, denationalised, and live somewhere or anywhere as a tolerated guest. But the historical will of the individual can only prove effective through identification with his own particular State. No one can change his nationality without suffering for it. If he feels constrained thereto, even though he does not necessarily forfeit the possibility of being himself or forfeit his consciousness of destiny, he will nevertheless forfeit the power of expansion through participation in the whole out of which he has grown in his own real world.

War and Peace. Because the power of the State is not a unique entity but is confronted at any time with a number of contemporaneous State individuals, and because there are implicit within it other possibilities of organisation than those which prevail at any particular time, its power manifests itself as the actual use of force whenever its unity is impaired. War and revolution are limits imposed upon the provision of the elementary necessaries of human life, and as their outcome that provision is placed upon new foundations of effectiveness and of law. Though all that is possible be done in order to avoid them, they loom as eventualities and constitute the unsolved problem menacing all life. If people adopt the principle of peace at any price, they will stumble along blindly and fall into an abyss when manœuvred by others into a situation in which, unless they fight, they will be destroyed or enslaved. Even if, short of pacifist extremism, everything possible is to be done in order to avoid war, still the harshness of reality demands that from moment to moment we shall be ready to reckon with the likelihood of war, and that we shall never forget what "at all costs" really signifies.

War being force in one of its most concrete developments, in war destiny speaks through physical clashes along the lines of preconsidered political resolves. It implies willingness to give one's life for one's faith in the unconditional value of one's own being; a firm conviction that it is better to die than to be a slave. The more fully the fighter realises what is at stake, the more effectively possible is such enthusiasm. But the more remote from facts the will to war, the more do high impulses tend to degenerate into feelings of a false romanticism.

To-day war seems to have undergone a change of meaning, insofar as it is not a war of religion but a war of interests, not a war of conflicting cultures or civilisations but a war of national areas, not a war of human beings but a technical struggle of machines one against another and all against the non-combatant population. It no longer appears as if in war human nobility were fighting on behalf of its future. War does not nowadays lead to any great historical decisions as did the victory of the Greeks over the Persians (which has remained as the foundation of the existence of the western personality down to our own time), or as the victory of the Romans over the Carthaginians, which safeguarded that same personality. If the result of a war is to change nothing, but only to destroy, with the mere result that a group of human beings who do not differ notably from the conquered acquires preponderant advantages for the future, there is lacking the affective strength of an existence that has inspired faith, of an existence whose destiny would have been decided by the war. Since to hazard one's life is not of itself a thing of intrinsic value, during the last war there ensued a peculiar solidarity among the soldiers engaged in a life-and-death struggle; there was a community in endurance, each man having to face his adversary, and to endure being sacrificed. Tenacity amid the persistent dangers of incalculable and overwhelmingly powerful chances, demands, at times, the display of presence of mind and resolution. Manliness in this situation created a peculiar heroism, incomparable in history. But that very manliness repudiates the responsibility for bringing about a situation in which every one will be forced back into war. Hence the cry, "Never again!"

But the horizon lours, and there seems no guarantee that the European nations will cease to make war on one another. The possibility of peace, on whose behalf many are working, might perhaps become actual because the technical advances in offensive weapons make the prospect of a European war so disastrous, and because, if the nations were at grips again, even the victorious aggressor would be ruined. But there still remains open the possibility of a new war which, more dreadful than any that have preceded it, would make an end of contemporary Europeans. Even if the reasons for war that are subject to economic control and regulation by treaty were supposed to be annulled, it is questionable whether there does not exist in man an obscure and blind will to make war; an impulse towards change, towards emergence from the familiarities of everyday life and from the stabilities of well-known conditions—something like a will to death as a will to annihilation and self-sacrifice, a vague enthusiasm for the upbuilding of a new world. Perhaps, even, there exists a romantically chivalrous love of battle for its own sake, or, it may be, a self-assertive impulse which seeks issue in the determination to show how much can be endured, and prefers a death freely chosen at the end of a life that has scarcely been found worth living, to a death passively envisaged. This passion may slumber awhile, to become active from time to time when the memory of the realities of war grows pale. If there lurk in man certain elements of invincible evil, then the task of the true leader would be, not merely to carry on a pacifist campaign against war in its direct aspect, but also to work against its menacing causes, to the end that a lengthy period of peace shall give possibilities of space and time for development. He should not strive for peace at any price, but should continue to work against the evil spirit of war even when, through a concatenation of circumstances, war has become impossible to prevent—endeavouring deliberately to fulfil war with the intrinsic value of a historically relevant decision. He should strive to ensure that out of war, which as such is rooted only in evil and in blind chance, true destiny shall emerge.

We are forced to assume, first that there is no immediate likelihood of the definitive establishment of peace or even of a war that shall have historically intrinsic value, and, secondly, that, despite this, man will remain placed in a situation of tension between the life-order and force. The vicious circle of dread of war which leads the nations to arm themselves for self-protection, with the result that bloated armaments ultimately lead to the war which they were intended to avert, can be broken in either of two conceivable ways. There might arise a unique world power, brought into being by the unification of all those now in possession of weapons, and equipped with the capacity to forbid the lesser and unarmed nations to make war. On the other hand, it may arise by the working of a fate to us still inscrutable which, out of ruin, will disclose a way towards the development of a new human being. To will the discovery of this way would be blind impotence, but those who do not wish to deceive themselves will be prepared for the possibility.

There remains for consideration the question of physical fitness for warfare. Even if we suppose peace to be established for an indefinite period, he will in the long run be lost who no longer possesses the internal readiness for physical struggle. What was forced upon Germany, namely a professional army in conjunction with the abolition of universal military service, signifies, should it be generalised, the greatest possible danger to peace, and the greatest menace to the likelihood of a war having intrinsic historical value —for it carries with it the renunciation of war by the masses with the undesired upshot that some day or another they will be enslaved by the minority of professional soldiers. The possibility of war will not be avoided by the fact that a vast majority of the population is no longer subjected to military training.

Even though military enthusiasm for war has become insincere, still the contemporary mental situation is such (in view of the bitter earnest of the unavoidable) as to demand the encouragement and the realisation of that form of fitness and willingness to bear arms without which all other goods would be lost. He who, faced by the hubbub and confusion of military oratory and by the instinct of impulsive confusion in anxious flight from reality, could still maintain clear vision and untroubled courage, and could discover the way towards physical fitness and willingness to bear arms along which others would follow him, would be the creator of the human substance which would sustain the future. In no case would it be a purely military courage, for this would be no more than a trustworthy element of the profounder courage of one willing to collaborate in a knowledge of the whole, and able to act from a sense of responsibility clarified by that knowledge—with force underlying it as a possibility but not as a necessity.

The situation would seem to make it indispensable to take sides actively, even during peace-time, in the mental struggle for or against war. Nevertheless, in view of the incomprehensible whole of human destiny, this alternative cannot be enforced, unless the peace of all be ensured by the power of one supreme authority —if this authority be accepted. The actual difficulty is that there are mystifications on both sides. The military pageantry intended to arouse a will to war does not reveal the condition of the population during gas-attacks, nor yet starvation, nor yet the way belligerents and non-belligerents die in war-time. The pacificists' arguments, on the other hand, refrain from disclosing what it means to become enslaved, or to live in accordance with the principles of non-resistance.

Both the militarists and the pacificists hide the sub-stratum of evil which is the obscure upshot of all the forces that finally discharge themselves in war—the way in which people come to regard their own lives as unquestionably more important than those of others, and as the only true things in the world; their inca-pacity for putting themselves in others' places without betraying their own selves; the fear which craves for safety, and can find it only in having a force that out-matches all others; the longing for power; insincerity towards oneself and others, so that life becomes a hopeless confusion, owing to the blind maintenance of ill-considered opinions, to guidance by unchallenged passion, until there seems no way out but resort to force. Our humanity is not, properly speaking, real, but exists only under certain conditions, and when these are in abeyance the savagery of animal selfishness manifests itself as life seeking to maintain itself at any cost to others. This happens as between man and man in moments of terrible self-revelation; and it happens likewise, at such moments, as between States.

In days to come it is possible that individual fitness for actual warfare might be reduced to near the vanish-ing-point, for, in the inter-relationships between States, there exists power which can rule without exercising the form of dominion and without any striking display of military means. States ostensibly sovereign are really dependent one upon another. It is questionable whether to-day world dominion could be acquired and exercised as of old. What has seemed a matter of course may become indifferent to history. Still, some-where or other will persist the point at which the whole will have at least the possibility of the victorious employment of force.

In this situation, one who has entered into cognisance of the whole will, in war, either collaborate at some historically relevant position (that is to say on behalf of the bringing of a true human existence into being), or else will not fight politically at all. Peripheral troubles, which result only in destruction or are without historical significance, remain beneath his dignity. An unconditional venture of one's life is only possible when a true human existence is at stake, that is to say on behalf of a genuinely historical destiny, and not where the matter concerns nothing more than the interests of national areas and economic corporations.

Yet reality makes other demands. What the whole is, over and above the extant perspective in a situation, remains incomprehensible. To-day we shall scarcely find it possible to believe what Schiller and Hegel used to believe, that universal history is a sort of world-assize. Realisation in failure can be just as real as realisation in success. No one can know what is given the preference on the transcendental plane.

Methods and Sphere of Influence of Political Activity. The methods of political activity that precede the direct use of force consist in training the will in such a way as to bring the masses into a unity. But in mass apparatuses every outstanding will has a peculiar incomprehensibility. Owing to the tension between leaders and masses, there is a tendency for each side to paralyse the other at the moment when either of them is about to take effective action.

The essential problem of the political history of our time is whether the masses of mankind can be democratised, whether average human nature is such as to enable each to accept his share of responsibility as a citizen equally aware with all others of what he is doing, and ready as a part of his daily life to take his share in deciding fundamental political issues. There can be no doubt that at the present day the vast majority of the electors do not record their votes as the outcome of conviction based upon sound knowledge, but that they are influenced by unverifiable illusions and by insincere promises; that the result of elections depends to a large extent upon the fact that there are such numerous abstentions; that fluctuating minorities, bureaucracies, or individuals whom chance has thrust into a prominent position, really rule. The masses can only decide anything by a majority vote. The sole path to dominion would appear to lead by way of a struggle to secure a majority at the polls by means of propaganda, suggestion, humbug, and the advocacy of private interests.

A genuine leader, one able to guide because his life has continuity and because he can form trustworthy decisions, only has a chance of leading when circumstances are favourable. The burning questions are: What does the leader appeal to in the masses? What instincts are stimulated, and for what kinds of efficiency is there scope? What sort of characters are excluded? He whose political will takes a particular trend must make the masses will the same thing as he does. These masses may be a minority. But leaders who enjoy the confidence of the masses to such an extent as enables them to undertake independent action are rarely encountered to-day. The leaders of our time are apt to be regarded with distrust, so that they can act only subject to control and to provisos, or as the exponents of the transient will of the masses, though they cease to be leaders when this will changes; or, their true character being for a time unrecognised, they are no more than successful demagogues able to intoxicate the masses; or, as leaders of a minority with which they have joint interests, they manage to get control of that military authority whereby all others than this minority are subjugated whether they like it or not.

When leadership is of such a kind, and during a period when the mass-order has been rendered absolute and when it is dominated by technique and economics, the State passes under the control of tendencies which run counter to and annul its essential idea. In some cases, therefore, the State, as an enterprise which is utterly chaotic as far as its spiritual life is concerned, becomes a mere unification of the rational life-order of the masses with that power in default of which nothing in the world can exist. Then, since the sense of the State has fallen into decay, the realities of State-power assume the form of chance decisions and of aimless modifications in the use of force. In other instances, as a reaction against this decay, the State-will becomes a dictatorial re-establishment of unity, authority, and obedience, as a result of which (the sense of the State having become fanatical in its intensity) human liberty will be lost, and there will remain nothing but the force of crude brutality. As a result of either of these transformations, leadership will become an embodiment of force which will lack the justification of a being intensified to the level of true humanity.

Thus the political destiny of all would seem to be a lack of destiny, for destiny only exists when selfhood grasps life, takes life over by its activity, realises itself, and dares. The sphere of influence of political activity appears to-day to be nothing more than the field on which the nature of humanity is to be historically decided. But this mental situation confronts every possible selfhood with the demand to attain to a knowledge of what it is possible to do upon the basis of a knowledge of what actually happens.

The sphere of influence of concrete activity, moreover, is no longer one of direct simplicity that it was during the struggle among the European States. An infinitely complicated world only a fraction of which becomes partially comprehensible to the individual after many years of experience and research, and a world with vague fighting fronts of which the combatants are not yet fully aware, is a world in which, in the lack of expert knowledge, action cannot but be clumsy and ineffective. Nothing but full clarity concerning a situation which is perpetually changing and regenerating itself under stress of action, can make action purposive and effective.

When, to conclude, no one can any longer continue to act for an extended period, but even the mightiest statesman derives his authority from the will of a temporary majority and loses it when the majority disappears, he necessarily guides his course with an eye to the effect of his actions upon the favour of the electors, being responsible, not to his God, but to the impalpable masses. He has to reckon with other men of might who are in a similar situation. The sphere of influence of political activity, therefore, is manifest in the methods of action and is but vaguely delimited. The Peace Conference at Versailles was symptomatic of the general condition of the world. Thanks to an unprecedented mechanism of communication, transport, and the transmission of news, the whole world, with the exception of Germany, was present at this conference. The forces of public opinion gave rise to tumultuous frictions wherein chance supplemented the skill of the negotiators, and

weariness at the interminable sittings led to the accept-
ance of results which fell far short of what some of
the leading spirits had wanted. The results were
accepted since, but for this, there was risk of a complete breakdown. President Wilson had wished to
create a new world-order, and sustained a decisive
defeat, because, being incompetent as a wire-puller,
he tried to hold rigidly to abstract principles, bringing about a state of affairs which was nicknamed a
"job-lot of idealism".

2. EDUCATION

Significance of Education. Man is not what he is
solely in virtue of biological inheritance, but also, and
much more, thanks to what tradition makes him.
Education is a process recapitulated in each individual.
Through the working of the factual historical world
in which the individual grows up, in conjunction with
the purposive education to which he is subjected
by parents and school, and in conjunction likewise
with the influence of the various institutions of social
life, to which, finally, there is super-added the effect
of all that he hears and experiences—he acquires that
which, elaborated by the activity of his own being,
is known as his culture, which becomes for him, so
to say, his second nature.

Culture brings the individual, by way of his own
being, into cognisance of the whole. Instead of stay-
ing fixed in one particular place, he goes out into the
world, so that, though his life be cast in narrow circumstances, it is still animated by contact with the
lives of all. A man can become more decisively himself in proportion to the clarity and richness of the
world with which his own reality becomes unified.

When the substance of the whole is unquestionably

present, education, linked with stable forms, has a self-evident value. It denotes the earnestness with which each successive generation is absorbed into the spirit of the whole as the culture out of which experience, work, and action proceed. The personal achievement of the educator is, as such, barely conscious. He serves a cause without making experiments; swims in the stream of mankind in the making —a stream which, as a rule, has a regular and continuous flow.

But when the substance of the whole has become questionable and is in a state of disintegration, education, too, becomes insecure and disintegrated. No longer does it bring children into touch with the greatness of an all-embracing whole, but has vague and multifarious results. Disquiet prevails throughout the world. Feeling that they are slipping down into fathomless abysses, people recognise that everything turns on what can be made of the coming generation. They know that education will determine the human existence of the future, and that a decay of education would mean the decay of mankind. But education decays when, in the individual human beings who, at their maturity, have to bear responsibility, the historically transmitted substance has crumbled. Anxiety about this substance is tantamount to a consciousness that there is peril of its being absolutely lost. In such circumstances, a man will look backwards, and will have his children taught as absolute that which he himself no longer regards as such. Another will reject this historical tradition, and will have education carried on as if it had no relationship with time at all, and consisted only of training for technical skill, the acquisition of realist knowledge, and information that will enable a child to take up a position towards the contemporary world. Every one knows that he who moulds children moulds the future.

Symptomatic of the uneasiness of our own age concerning education is the intensity of pedagogical efforts in the absence of any unified ideas upon the subject, the superabundance of new books on education, the perpetual amplification of the didactic art. Nowadays the individual teacher is a more self-sacrificing person than ever before, and is nonetheless, because he is not sustained by a whole, practically impotent. Moreover, it seems as if the characteristic feature of our situation was the breaking-up of substantial education into an interminable pedagogic experiment, its decomposition into indifferent possibilities. The freedoms which men have wrung for themselves are being dissipated in the futile liberty of the null. One attempt is speedily abandoned in favour of another, the contents, aims, and methods of education being changed from moment to moment. An epoch which does not trust its own self is anxiously concerned about education as if in this domain something could once more be made out of nothing.

Characteristic is the part played by young people. When education is substantial because it proceeds from the spirit of a whole, youth is immature. It venerates, obeys, trusts, and does not claim validity as youth; for it is no more than preparatory and the possible mission of a future. But when things are in a state of dissolution, youth acquires a value *per se*. We actually turn to youth expecting it to supply us with what has been lost from the world. It is considered entitled to regard itself as an original source. Already our children are allowed to have a say in the ordering of the school. It seems as if young folk were demanding the right to produce for themselves what their teachers no longer possess. Just as the coming generations are burdened with the national debt of earlier days, so will they have to bear the consequences of our squandering of mental goods, which they will have to reacquire for themselves. Youth is endowed with a fictitious preponderance, and misses its purpose for the reason that man can only become man if he grows in the continuity of decades and is strictly guided into the right path by a succession of footsteps which he has to follow.

When, after such an education, in the medley of the indifferent and the chance-given, the adult has not succeeded in making his way into a world, but is left forsaken and becomes aware of the fact, there arises, as a sign of the times, a demand for adult education. Formerly, as far as grown-ups were concerned, there was only a question of the diffusion of knowledge into wider circles; the only problem was the possibility of popularisation. To-day the burning question is whether it will be possible, out of the sources of contemporary life, not to dilute the old culture, but to establish a new one in the community of popular educators, workers, employees, and peasants. Man in his forlornness is not merely to accommodate himself by comprehending reality, but is once more to belong to a community which, transcending occupation and party, will bring human beings together as such; men are once again to become a nation. Whatever doubts we may entertain as to the feasibility of adult education in this sense, we must not fail to recognise the serious importance of the proposed task. If all our old ideals are to be shattered upon the realities of the times, the attempt to rise superior to the situation may perhaps be foredoomed to failure, but the mere endeavour shows a vestige of human dignity. If there no longer exists a nation, a people, in which the individual feels a self-evident appurtenance (or if this nation or people remains only in fragments), if, in the inexorable process of dissolution, everything is merged in the masses—then, no doubt, it is no more than utopian romanticism to long for the up-building of a new people. Still, the longing is justified. Meanwhile, however, there exists nothing but comradeship among friends, the manifest reality of a few persons endowed with a will to get into touch with those originally of another way of thinking. Hence the movement for adult education as at present understood is not reality, but a symptom of the forlornness of mankind in the cultural disintegration of an epoch when education has broken down.

The State and Education. The State, in virtue of its power, is the guarantor of the extant form of mass-order.

The masses do not really know what they want. Mass-demands relate to average matters, as capable of being expressed in the crudest terms. When the demands of the masses determine the nature of education, the upshot is something of this kind. People want to learn what will be practically applicable in life: they want to keep in close contact with life, and understand (in this connexion) by "life" all that makes life easy and comfortable, not excepting the means of communication in the great cities; they want to cultivate individuality, denoting by this, on the one hand, utility (which they miscall "efficiency"), and, on the other hand, insubordination, this meaning a licence to give rein to every inclination and to take pleasure in doing what all of like ways of thinking do (which they term "being natural"); they protest against the stringency of ideal aims, for these demand gradations of being instead of mere utility; they want individuals who can live together without friction, and they deny the possibility of essentially responsible human beings.

The State, being the framework in which the permanent education of all can be carried on, is concerned about the education of youth. For, thanks to education, there are produced the human beings who will in due course have to sustain the State.

To-day it would seem that two widely differing possibilities are open to the State.

On the one hand, it may leave education alone, may let the mass-demands take their own course, and may try, in conflict with them, to work out an aristocratic educational system of its own. In these circumstances it will dominate without any kind of unification or stability by means of its personal policy, which will result in a distribution of the leading educational positions among the dominant parties. Multiplicity of curricula and of educational experiments will be tolerated to the extent of utter disintegration, restricted only by this consideration, that nothing can be established which does not, in the long run, secure the support of a powerful political group. Here and there a school may thrive thanks to the personality of its headmaster, if he be allowed free choice in the appointment of his assistant masters. On the whole, however, the result will be that the teachers will all be at sixes and sevens, failing to understand one another, harnessed to mechanical curricula, in schools where no genuine community spirit prevails, but subject to guidance by empty rhetoric of one sort or another—nationalist, philosophical, or social. Continuity is rendered impossible by reciprocal interference. Everything is higgledy-piggledy, and there are continual changes. Children fail to receive the sincere, great, noble impressions which are able to influence character in a way that can never be forgotten. Immense demands are made upon the young as regards the acquisition of facts, so that immature minds are strained whilst no imprint is effected upon their real being. There is a lack of straightforward objectivity which, upon the foundation of a belief, would energetically resist the subjectivity of the individual capacity or incapacity. More is done to develop individuality than is desirable, and yet the teacher fails to achieve what he strives to achieve—namely, the formation of character. Torn hither and thither, the child finds, indeed, fragments of a tradition, but no world into which it can confidently enter.

If the alternative plan is followed, the State acquires control of education for the quiet but forcible moulding of character in accordance with its own purposes. Then we have a unified education at the cost of paralysis of mental freedom. Basic opinions are inculcated with the fixity of religious dogmas, knowledge and accomplishments being drilled into the learner as ways of feeling and valuing. What the bolsheviks and the fascists respectively do in this field and what we learn of the decline of liberty in the United States, differ in respect of many points of detail—but, common to them all, is that human beings are turned out according to standardised types.

The masses are aware of this imposition of uniformity by the force of the State, and they are aware of an aimless multiplicity. But if education is once more to become what it was in its best days, namely the possibility, through historical continuity, of developing into a human being possessed of full selfhood, that can only ensue through a faith which, amid all necessary strictness in learning and practice, indirectly conveys a spiritual value.

No simple recipe can be given for this. Here the power of the State cannot create anything, but can only protect or destroy. It is the mental situation which imposes its demands when, contemplating the future, we become aware of the whole. Education will only be restored to its true level when the valuations of the masses are overridden by a distinction between teaching and discipline, between that which is comprehensible to all, and that which is attainable by an élite through a training of the inner being.

3. INCOMPREHENSIBILITY OF THE WHOLE

If the whole be thought of as a world-wide reality, then there becomes valid the idea of a general condition of all human beings or of restricted masses of human beings as the general interest. In various projects this general interest manifests itself in primarily heterogeneous forms: as the utopia of a sound system for the provision of the elementary necessaries of life for the masses under conditions of perpetual peace; as the metaphysic of a being of the State *per se*, which everything else has to serve; as a frame of mind in which a general approval is given to the idea of a movement that will change the world through the operation of the forces now actually working upon it, without any attempt to forecast the future (for the trends of the movement will only be disclosed in an unpredictable future); as a frame of mind of self-restriction on the part of the State and the social apparatus in favour of inviolable human rights and in favour of lacunæ which will leave space for the possible selfhood of the individual in its manifold developments; as the historical life of a national people.

These forms come into conflict upon the mental plane, and are grounds for the activation of previously obscure motives. But each one of them is false insofar as it claims to be valid as an abstract generality. Political activity, rather, is always found to take place as the outcome of a concrete historical situation in an inscrutable whole; every person, every group, and every State exists in some particular place, and not everywhere at once; whatever occurs has only its own particular possibility, and not that of mankind at large. Political activity is the reality which the whole wills and decides. It is in a condition of ultimate dependence, which remains to it incomprehensible, whether as the aggregate of reality or as the transcendental.

But what makes the metamorphosis from the vague to the genuinely effective will to political action extraordinarily difficult is the fact that the fighting fronts in the State and in the relationships between the various States are to-day so vague.

For example, the people as an aggregate about whose being political action is concerned has to-day become questionable, and yet has not been altogether thrust off the stage. Nationalist movements throughout the world are more intolerant than ever, and yet in them "nation" is nothing more than the existence of a common speech in conjunction with a levelling type. Nation ceases to be conformable with people or folk in the genuine sense of the term when it is forced into the unfreedom of this kind of self-consciousness. Conversely, many reject nationality as the false front of interests to which they are alien in order to cling to unhistorical ties between kindred masses believed to exist in all peoples.

Both the nationalised people and the vague mass of the people for whom the elementary necessaries of life have to be provided suppress the selfhood which was originally connected with the obscure foundations of the people. No longer can any one who thinks clearly participate on this fighting front. He who earnestly wishes to participate in man's destiny must get to work upon a deeper level. The historical continuity of one's own being in the mental tradition upon the foundation of a hereditary succession does not exist as a simple datum; it becomes actual only as a power of selfhood when it is freely assumed and appropriated. Modern man is in a terrible situation when he can no longer have faith in his own people in the form with which it is endowed by its contemporary objectivity and in which it manifests its demands, but has to plumb the depths out of which he may, perhaps, bring to the surface the substantial historical continuity of his being—or may sink into the fathomless abyss.

Destiny cannot be coerced in accordance with an ideal. It first becomes manifest in the concrete historical situation. That which is historically given is a substance which, since the days of the French Revolution, men have inclined to believe themselves able to break away from altogether. It is as if a man were deliberately to saw off the branch upon which he is sitting. We fancy ourselves to have become enabled to grasp our whole life by dealing with it purposively. But two alternative dangers arise: first, that of undermining our life in the attempt to organise it rightly as a whole; and, secondly, that of laying ourselves fast amid unprecedented coercions whose existence we recognise but which we find ourselves constrained to endure. Every attempt to break away from our history has, however, proved a failure for the reason that (fortunately for our mental stability) history reasserts its rights in some new form. To understand the present moment in universal history is the task of political construction, proceeding from a concrete situation. Politics regarded as the self-seeking calculation of a particular State implies that all other States are regarded, as circumstances vary, in the light of possible allies or possible enemies, interchangeable at will. A State will enter into an alliance with a most alien power against those powers that are intellectually and historically nearest to it. If Britain, for instance, were to become involved in a war with the United States, she would unhesitatingly join forces with Japan. Britain and France brought Indian and Senegalese troops to the Rhine. It is unlikely that Germany would refuse to make common cause with Russia if this would give her a good chance of regaining her freedom.

On the other hand even to-day those whose politics are sustained by a historical consciousness of the whole, look beyond the interests of any individual State towards the coming interests of human existence at large, which are vaguely foreshadowed in the contrast between the western and the Asiatic nature, between European freedom and Russian fanaticism. They do not forget the profoundly human and spiritual ties that unite the German nature with that of the Anglo-Saxon and with that of the Latin nations; and they shrink from the treachery which is being continually perpetrated.

It is impossible to foresee where the fighting fronts of the future will be situated; or, rather, any possible way of imagining them is absurd because the actual fighting front apparent at any moment can never conform to the inward significance of human existence fighting for its future.

The whole is a tension of incompatibles. It is not for us an object, but is, upon a far and vague horizon, the habitat of human beings as self-dependent existences, of their creation as visible formations, of the clarification of the suprasensual in the sensual—all sinking back once more into the abyss of non-existence.

It may be that the freedom of human beings can only endure and that the experience of their being can only undergo indefinite expansion, on the proviso that this tension shall never be resolved. Dictatorships and a reliable apparatus for the supply of the elementary needs of the masses, lead to the establishment of a mechanised system in which man as man can no longer exist. One possible form of a unified solution may be the yearning that arises from our need for tranquillity. But what we really ought to wish for, if possible, is that what we are striving for as a solution shall, after all, never be achieved. In the political field there obtains the paradox that that must not be perfected which with our utmost energy we are striving to perfect.

Upon the educational field the state of affairs is the same as in the realm of politics. Education is dependent upon something that at once overrides it and is its source—upon the life of a spiritual world. Education cannot derive from itself, but serves for the transmission of the life which manifests itself directly in human behaviour; for it has deliberately adopted an attitude towards the reality of the system that provides the elementary necessities of human life and towards the State, and it soars upwards through the appropriation of whatever is created on the mental plane. The destiny of the mind in our epoch must determine the value of such education as is still possible.

If the soul vanishes from the State and from education, if there is lacking the will which, arising out of the unconditioned, acts as arbiter in the realm of historical continuity, and if both are hopelessly subjected to the chaotic oscillation between rational planning and the irrational use of force, these are indications that the efficacy of the overriding whole is extinct or is at any rate in abeyance for a time. But when this efficacy gives man a consciousness of grip and of meaning, then its being manifests itself in the impossibility of completing or resolving the temporarily extant world-organisation.

The leap from the State and education to the whole of mind, human existence, and transcendentalism, is not the leap to a reality actually existing in the world, but the leap into another reality, existentially on a higher plane though in actual manifestation entirely dependent—a reality which nevertheless, at critical moments, determines the course of things as that of manifest reality.

PART THREE

DECAY AND POSSIBILITIES OF THE MIND

WE saw that the State, as a living reality, was the limit at which something which is more than life itself determines life through the will in the whole. Whereas, however, the State is, in virtue of its power, the supreme authority for decisions in life, it is not supreme for the human being himself. The State does not come to rest in the human being. Even when the State identifies itself with the human being, to the latter the whole still remains questionable; inasmuch as, for the human being, the State remains nothing more than an intermediate entity in the perpetual movement through time. If, therefore, the State, degraded to become a mere servant of the mass-order, has lost all relationship to true destiny, and if, in this condition of dependence, it betrays the possibilities of the human being as existence in labour, occupational work, mental creation, then man, as selfhood, must, in his inner being, take up a position even against the State. It is true that the life-order existent through the power of a State can never be surrendered or sacrificed, for therewith everything would go to ruin; but a life in radical opposition to the State may arise, under stress of the fundamental question how the conquest of the life-order is once more to be achieved.

Since man can find no completion in the realisation

of his life as a whole, soaring above life, he builds for himself a second world, the world of the mind, in the space wherein he becomes fully aware of himself in the general form of his being. No doubt, as a mental being likewise, he is fast bound to the realities of his life, but in this soaring flight he transcends life. Cutting loose, for a moment, from mere reality, he finds his way back into the being that he has become through the visions and the creations of his mind.

Thus originating, the second world is fashioned and discovered in the first. By attaining to a knowledge of his being, man is able to transcend life as a datum. By means of his culture, he consummates the mental process into which the extant machinery for the provision of the elementary necessaries of human life is converted in virtue of the significance of the idea that permeates it. The mind creates a language for itself in art, science, and philosophy.

The destiny of the mind subsists in the polarity of dependent life on the one hand and originality on the other. It is lost alike in mere dependence and in an imaginary unreality. Even when the reality of life has been sustained by an ideal, this ideal can fade, and that which had been mind, may continue to exist as a residue, as an accessory, as a mask, as nothing more than a stimulant.

In our epoch of the mass-order, of technique, of economics, when an attempt is made to render this inevitable institution absolute, there is a danger to the selfhood that the fundamental basis of the mind may be destroyed. Just as the State as man's ally may be paralysed, so also can the mind be paralysed, when it ceases to function sincerely in virtue of its own origin and is falsified through subservience to the masses and by working in subordination to the finite purposes of these.

1. CULTURE

Culture is a form of life; its backbone is mental discipline, the ability to think; and its scope is an ordered knowledge. As its substance it has a contemplation of the forms of that which has existed, cognition as coercively valid insight, a knowledge of things, and familiarity with words.

Culture and the Antique. For the broad masses of the population in the West, culture has hitherto been successful only along the path of humanism; but for individuals other roads have been opened. He who in youth has learned Greek and Latin, has absorbed the writings of the classical poets, philosophers, and historians, has gained familiarity with mathematics, has studied the Bible and some of the great imaginative writers of his own country, will have entered into a world which, in its infinite mobility and expanse, will have endowed him with an inalienable intrinsic value, and will have given him the key to other worlds. But such education is, in virtue of its realisation, simultaneously a selection. Not every one who tries can unlock this treasure-house. Many fail to do so, and acquire nothing more than superficialities. What is decisive is not a specific talent for languages or for mathematics or for the elements of a modern culture, but a readiness to receive mental impressions. A humanist education is that which exerts a selective influence upon the individual. Only this education, therefore, has the wonderful quality of being able to produce good results even though the teachers are inefficient. One who reads the *Antigone*, and who revolts, in this connexion, against being taught nothing but grammar and prosody, may still be profoundly impressed because the text lies before him.

If we inquire why this task of humanistic culture has such remarkable advantages, an answer can only be found on historical lines, and not with reference to any rational purposiveness of a humanist education. The actual fact is that we owe to the classical world the foundation of what, in the West, makes man all that he can be. In Hellas the idea of culture was for the first time fully realised and understood in a way that, ever since, has been valid for every person of understanding. In the West, each great uplift of selfhood has been brought about by a fresh contact with the classical world. When that world has been forgotten, barbarism has always revived. Just as a boat cut loose from its moorings drifts aimlessly hither and thither at the mercy of the winds and the waves, so do we drift when we lose touch with the antique. Our primary foundation, changeable though it may be, is invariably the classical world; for the past of our own particular nation is effective only to a secondary extent and lacks an independent cultural energy. We are citizens of the western world through our dependence upon a nationality which has become positive in virtue of a specific appropriation of classicism. To-day, however, this classical culture is, in the best event, as far as the masses are concerned, merely tolerated. The number of persons to whom it really means something grows continually smaller.

A Levelling-Down of Culture ; Specialised Capacity. In the life of the mass-order, the culture of the generality tends to conform to the demands of the average human being. Spirituality decays through being diffused among the masses when knowledge is impoverished in every possible way by rationalisation until it becomes accessible to the crude understanding of all. As a result of the levelling-down process characteristic of the mass-order, there is a tendency towards the disappearance of that stratum of cultured persons who have come into being thanks to a continuous disciplining of their thoughts and feelings so that they have been rendered capable of mental creation. The mass-man has very little spare time, does not live a life that appertains to a whole, does not want to exert himself except for some concrete aim which can be expressed in terms of utility; he will not wait patiently while things ripen; everything for him must provide some immediate gratification; and even his mental life must minister to his fleeting pleasures. That is why the essay has become the customary form of literature, why newspapers are taking the place of books and why desultory reading has been substituted for the perusal of works that can serve as an accompaniment to life. People read quickly and cursorily. They demand brevity; not the brevity, the terseness, which can form the starting-point of serious meditation, but the brevity which swiftly provides what they want to know and furnishes data which can be as swiftly forgotten. No longer is the reader in mental communion with what he reads.

Culture now signifies something which never acquires a form, but is to emerge with extraordinary intensity out of a vacancy into which there is a speedy return. The associated estimates of value are typical. Men are quickly satiated with what they have heard, and are therefore ever on the search for novelties since nothing else tickles their fancy. Novelties are acclaimed as the primal knowledge of which people are in search; but they are whistled down the wind a moment after, since all that is wanted is sensation.

Being fully aware that he lives in an epoch when a new world is in process of formation and a world in which the past no longer counts, he who craves for novelty is continually prattling of the "new" as if, because novel, it must necessarily be effective. He speaks of "new thought", a "new sense of life", the "new physical culture", a "new objectivity", the "new economics", etc. If anything be "new", it must be of positive value; if it be not "new", it is regarded as of little worth. Though a man has nothing whatever to say, he is still possessed of an understanding, and can, when difficulties arise, employ this simply as a force for resistance; and merely to be "intelligent" is considered to imply a mental capacity for true existence. People have no sense of close kinship with their fellows, can no longer love them but only make use of them, only have comrades and enemies on a plane of abstract theory or for the fulfilment of some obvious purpose. The individual is deemed "interesting" not for his own sake, but simply because he is stimulating; and the stimulus ceases to work as soon as he no longer surprises. When people describe any one as "cultured", all they mean is that he has the faculty of appearing new, intelligent, and interesting. The domain of this culture is discussion, which to-day has become a mass-phenomenon. Yet discussion, instead of furnishing the pleasure which finds expression in the three foregoing estimates, could only give true gratification if it were a genuine form of communication as the expression of a struggle of conflicting fates or as the imparting of experiences and cognitions belonging to a jointly constituted world.

The mass-diffusion of knowledge and of its expression leads to a wearing-out of words and phrases. In the cultural chaos that now exists, anything can be said, but only in such a way that it signifies nothing. The vagueness of the meaning of words, nay the renunciation of that true significance which first enables mind to enter into touch with mind, has made an essential mutual understanding impossible. When language is used without true significance, it loses its purpose as a means of communication and becomes an end in itself. Should I look at a landscape through a pane of glass, and should this pane of glass become clouded, I cease to see the landscape if my attention is directed towards the glass itself. To-day no attempt is made to use language as a means of contemplating being, language being substituted for being. Being is to be "original" or "primitive", so customary words are avoided, and especially words of a higher significance which might convey true values. Unfamiliar words and phrases are to create a semblance of primitive truth, of profundity dependent upon the use of novel terms. Mental capacity is supposed to be displayed by the renaming of things. For a moment the attention of the hearer is riveted by the surprising effect of the unfamiliar terminology, until the new word, likewise, has staled, or discloses itself as a mask. This concentration upon words for their own sake is the outcome of a convulsive endeavour to discover form in the cultural chaos. The upshot is that to-day the manifestation of culture is either an imperfectly understood and watered-down chatter in which any words you like are used; or else it is verbosity in place of reality, a mere fashion of speech. The fundamental significance of language for human existence has been transformed into a phantom by turning away the attention.

Amid this irresistible decomposition, there is an intensification of the cultural realities which disclose

paths of ascent. As far as precise occupational knowledge goes, expertise has become a matter of course.
Specialised ability of one sort and another is now
widely diffused; the relevant knowledge can be
acquired by a practical study of the methods concerned
and can be reduced to the simplest form in the way
of results. Throughout the extant chaos there are
cases in which people can display expertise. But this
expertise is dispersed; each individual is expert in
one thing only, and his faculty is often an extremely
restricted one, not being a manifestation of his true
being, nor yet brought into relation with the overriding whole as the unity of a cultivated consciousness.

Historical Appropriation or Assimilation. There has
arisen an enmity to culture which reduces the value
of mental activity to a technical capacity and to the
expression of the minimum of crude life. This attitude is correlative to the process of the technicisation
of the planet and of the life of the individual, wherein,
among all nations, there has been a breach in historical
tradition so that everything has been placed upon new
foundations. Nothing can continue to exist except
that which finds its technical rationale in the new
world created by the West, but which, though thus
"western" in its origin, is universally valid in its significance and its effects. Hence human existence has
been shaken to its roots. The disturbance, as far as
the West is concerned, is the most extensive that has
ever been experienced; but because it is the outcome
of the mental development peculiar to the West, it is
part of the continuity of the world to which it belongs.
In the case of other civilisations than the western,
however, it assails them from without as a catastrophe.
Nothing can persist in its traditional form. The great
civilised nations of India and of the Far East are con-

fronted by the same fundamental problem. They are compelled to undergo a transformation which will adapt them to the world of technical civilisation with its sociological causes and consequences, for in default of this they will perish. Whilst an enmity to culture is grinding to powder all that has hitherto existed (with an arrogant assumption that the world is now beginning entirely afresh), in the process of reconstitution the mental substance can only be preserved by a sort of historical remembrance which must be something more than a mere knowledge of the past and must take the form of a contemporary vital force. In default of this, man would slip back into barbarism. The overwhelming radicalness of the crisis of our era pales before the eternal substance in whose being memory participates as in the immortal elements common to all times.

Hostility to the past, therefore, is one of the birth-pangs of the new valuation of historicity. This historicity itself is at war with historism as a false historicity, insofar as it has become a spurious and substitute culture. For remembrance as a mere knowledge of the past is nothing more than a collection of an infinite number of antiquarian details; remembrance as mere contemplation instinct with understanding realises the pictures and the figures of the past only as a non-committal confrontation. It is not until remembrance takes the form of appropriation or assimilation that there comes into being the reality of the selfhood of a contemporary human being in the form of veneration; subsequently as a standard for his own feeling and activity; and finally as participation in his own eternal being. The problem of the mode of remembrance is the problem of such culture as still remains possible.

Everywhere, widely diffused institutions subserve our knowledge of the past. The extent to which the modern world is concerned about such institutions manifests a deep-lying instinct which, amid the general destruction of culture, nevertheless refuses to accept the possibility of a complete breach in historical continuity. The works of the past are preserved in museums, libraries, and archives, with the consciousness that something irreplaceable is being safeguarded, even though, for the moment, it be not properly understood. Men of all parties, all ways of thinking, and all nations make common cause to-day in this activity, whose watchful fidelity has never before been so widely generalised or taken so much as a matter of course. The vestiges of history are protected and cared for wherever possible. What of old times was great, lives on, so to say, as a mummy, and becomes an object of pilgrimage. Places which once played a great part in the world and realised the splendour of republican independence, are now kept going by an influx of foreign visitors. The whole of Europe has become, in a sense, a huge museum of the history of western mankind. In the trend towards historical commemorations, towards festivals recording the foundation of States, towns, universities, theatres, the birth and death of persons of note—remembrance, even though devoid of any fulfilment characterised by intrinsic worth, still discloses itself as a symptom of the will to preservation.

Only in exceptional individuals does witting remembrance pass over into a comprehensive intuition. It is as if man were forsaking the present and were going back to live in the past. What is over and done with, nevertheless persists as a cultural element devoid of content. The panorama of the millenniums is like a

138

region of beatific contemplation. During the nine-teenth century this attitude towards the past assumed an unprecedented expansiveness and objectivity. The passion for the contemplation of the past set people free from the miseries of the present; they felt happy while studying the great things which their forefathers had been able to achieve. Here was a cultural world which became metamorphosed into the tradition of a mere life in books and witnesses of the past. The epigones of the first contemplators handed down faded pictures of what their greater predecessors had seen. That which aforetime had been a primary vision of the great figures was preserved by epigones of the epigones, still fascinated by the work of a world reproduced in understanding, or at least in word and teaching.

But antiquarian lore and pictorial understanding can, in the last analysis, enjoy their rights only as guides to a contemporary possible realisation. The historical is appropriated or assimilated, not as a mere knowledge of something, not as a Golden Age which is to be restored because it should never have been allowed to fall into decay. Appropriation or assimilation occurs only through a rebirth of human existence by means of which the past is transformed thanks to the entry into a spiritual region wherein I became myself in virtue of my own originality. Culture through appro-priation of the past does not serve to destroy the present as something that is not worth while, in order that we may lightly escape it. The function of appropriation or assimilation is to enable me, by keeping my gaze fixed upon past altitudes, to find my way to the summit of a reality that is possible of achievement to-day.

That which is acquired as a new possession is some-thing which transforms the present. The insincere historicity of a culture which does no more than understand is a mere will to repeat the past; but a sincere historicity is a readiness to discover the sources which feed all life and therefore the life of the present as well. Then, without purpose or plan, there will ensue true appropriation; but the realising force of remembrance will be incalculable. The contemporary situation, with the attendant danger of a breach in the continuity of history, makes it necessary that we should deliberately grasp at the possibility of this remembrance. For if the breach were allowed to become established, man would destroy himself. When the rising generations enter into the machine-made world of the life-order of the masses, they find to-day, in an unprecedented abundance and accessibility, the instruments of remembrance in the form of books, statues, pictures, buildings, monuments, and various other works, not excepting the articles of daily use in the domestic life of old days—all as means for becoming aware of the fact of their own origin. The question arises: What can existence in its historicity make of all this?

Culture as a mere knowledge and understanding could romantically desire a re-establishment of the irrevocable, while forgetting that every historical situation knows only its own possibilities of realisation. Over against this stood the straightforwardness of a thrifty way of living which, in the region of the historically contemplated, desired only that which was unconditionally requisite for its activity. True culture would rather be itself in a minimum of appropriation than lose itself in the metamorphoses of a wider world. It would seem to be owing to this impulse that the sense for the straightforwardly sincere and for the existentially primitive has become effective as regards history as well as regards other things.

Once again decisive here is, not merely the worth of multiplicity, but also, and above all, the summits from which man speaks to all epochs. What is slight and small to-day becomes unified with what is great. The disillusionment which romantic enthusiasm has to encounter in the clash with the realities of contemporary life is transformed into the illusion-free contemplation of the genuine which was simultaneously bountiful.

The Press. Newspapers constitute the mental life of our day as the awareness of how things go with the masses. Though at first a simple handmaiden for the communication of views, the Press has now become dominant in the world. It creates a vital knowledge in a generally accessible definiteness as contrasted with expert knowledge which is accessible only to the connoisseur because couched in a terminology incomprehensible to those who lack specialised training. The articulation of this vital knowledge, arising as reports and disregarding the study of positive knowledge as a means of transition, comes into being as the anonymous culture of our era and as a culture still in process of creation. The newspaper as an idea embodies the possibility of a splendid realisation of the culture of the masses. It eschews vague generalities and aggregates of externals, in order to achieve a vivid, inconspicuously constructive, and pregnant presentation of the facts. It embraces all that happens in the realm of the mind, including even the remotest esoteric specialities and the most sublime personal creations. It seems to re-create, inasmuch as, by assembling the facts in close proximity, it brings into the consciousness of the times what otherwise would remain the ineffective possession of a few individuals. By the metamorphoses it achieves, it makes comprehensible to the generality what would otherwise remain intelligible only to professional persons. The literature of ancient times which, in comparison with our own, gave expression to a small, clear, and simple world, rendering it plastically visible to itself, might be taken as an example, and has been taken as an example by certain individuals. A *humanitas* which, with windows open in all directions, can contemplate things directly, is its essence. But, owing to the overwhelming complication of the facts of modern life, the claim of the world which wants to make itself known is radically different.

To discover amid the multifarious rubbish of what is printed from day to day the jewels of an amazingly terse and highly polished insight in the perfected speech of a simplified report, is an intense (if not a very frequent) gratification for modern man. These precious stones are the outcome of the mental discipline which here manifests itself and unnoticeably affects the consciousness of contemporary man. Our respect for the journalist increases when we make clear to ourselves the significance of his utterances for daily life. What happens in the present must not be grasped only by those to whom it becomes directly known; for the journalist's business is to make it appeal to hundreds of thousands. The momentary utterance has far-reaching effects. The word thus spoken is an achievement in the closest touch with life, determining, in part, the course of events, through modifying the ideas which human beings have in the mass. What is often deplored, insofar as the printed word fails to have a lasting and widespread effect on readers—the fact that the newspaper utterance is fugitive and ephemeral—can to-day, through the active participation of the readers, become a part of genuine reality. The journalist's position, therefore, is one of peculiar responsibility, which, anonymous though he be, should give him self-confidence and a keen sense of honour. He knows his power, amid the play of events, to control the levers that work in the heads of his fellow human beings. He becomes one of the collaborators in the creation of the present, inasmuch as he is able to say the right word here and now.

But his highest possibilities can lapse into demoralisation. True, there is no crisis affecting the Press. Its kingdom is assured. In this realm, the fight is not for the existence of its dominion, nor yet against those who used to be its adversaries, but is waged in order to decide whether the power of an independent contemporary mind shall continue vigorous or shall fall into decay. It may be regarded as unavoidable and as readily comprehensible that those who have to write and to think only for the moment should often write, though skilfully, in a hurry and without due consideration. The most disastrous feature of the position, however, is that the responsibility and the mental creativeness of journalism should be imperilled by the journalists having to be dependent upon the needs of the masses and upon politico-economical magnates. We are often told that a pressman cannot possibly remain mentally honourable. If he is to find a market for his wares, he must appeal to the instincts of the millions. Sensationalism, triviality, a careful avoidance of troubling his readers to use their intelligence, are likely to make what he writes frivolous and even debasing. If the Press is to pay, it must enter more and more into the service of political and economic powers. Under such controls, pressmen cultivate the art of deliberate lying and indulge in propaganda on behalf of matters repugnant to their higher selves.

They have to write to order. Only if the ruling powers of life were themselves sustained by an ideal, and only if the journalist could feel himself in harmony with these powers, would he be able to be perfectly sincere.

The origination of a caste with an ethic of its own, a caste which, in actual fact, exercises a mental dominance over the world, is the characteristic of our epoch. Its destiny is at one with that of the world. Without a press, the modern world could not exist. The upshot will depend, not only upon readers and the powers that be, but also upon the primary will of the human beings who, by their mental activity, give a stamp to the caste in question. The ultimate problem is whether mass-qualities will hopelessly ruin everything which, through the exercise of these possibilities, human beings might become.

The journalist can realise the ideal of the modern universalised man. He can merge himself in the tension and the reality of the day, adopting a reflective attitude towards these. He can seek out that innermost region where the soul of the age takes a step forward. He deliberately interweaves his destiny with that of the epoch. He takes alarm, he suffers, and he balks when he encounters nullity. He becomes insincere when he is content with that which brings satisfaction to the majority. He soars towards the heights when he sincerely fulfils his being in the present.

2. MENTAL CREATION

Mental work which seeks its field of activity in a concentration that disregards the momentary demands of the environment, takes long views. An individual goes out into the world to find what he can bring back from it. The very manner of this mental work would appear to-day to be threatened with decay. Just as under State socialism regarded as a means for supplying the elementary needs of the masses, economic interests mask the State or make a wrong use of the State for the advantage of individual types of property-holders, so does art become mere amusement and pleasure (instead of an emblem of the transcendental), science becomes concern for technical utility (instead of the satisfaction of a primary will to know), philosophy becomes a doctrinaire or hysterical and spurious knowledge (instead of man's very being safeguarded against the doubts and dangers of radical thought).

In almost all domains of activity there are brilliant achievements. Much is effected which can rightly be regarded as excellent, nay extraordinary. But, often enough, that which is achieved lacks the essence, the kernel, which, if present, would make something ostensibly less good really worth having.

The increase in mental possibilities seems to open unexampled prospects. Yet these possibilities appear to be undermined owing to more and more extensive provisos. The rising generation no longer assimilates the acquirements of earlier days. It looks as if human hands could no longer grasp the harvest of the past.

There is no trustworthy limitation by a whole which, prior to all work, can unconsciously point out the way to a self-dependent acquisition capable of being ripened. For centuries it has become plainer and plainer that the work of mental creation must be done by persons for whom the mainspring wells up from within. Throughout history, indeed, loneliness has been the foundation of all genuine activity; but this solitude was interrelated with the nation to which it historically belonged. To-day the mental creator has, it would seem, to live, not merely as a solitary, but as if he were making a fresh beginning, in touch with no one, apart alike from friends and from foes. Nietzsche was the first outstanding figure of whom this terrible loneliness was the dominant characteristic.

Unsustained by earlier generations or by the present generation, cut adrift from a really vital tradition, the mental creator can no longer be a member of a community of persons engaged in the possible perfectionment of a path. He does not take his steps nor draw his conclusions in an overriding environment. He is menaced by the haphazard, in which he cannot march boldly forward, but squanders his energies. The world does not impose on him any sort of mission. He must choose his course at his own risk. Without response, or only with a false response, and without a genuine adversary, he loses the necessary self-assurance. If he is to escape from this lack of concentration, he will need almost superhuman energy. In the absence of an unfaltering and lucid education, an education with a definite goal, an education thanks to which the highest becomes attainable, he will have to zigzag amid continuous losses, and will perhaps at the end begin to see the possibility of making a real start when the time for a start has slipped by! It is as if he had been deprived of breath, inasmuch as he is no longer surrounded by the world of mental reality out of which the individual must grow if he is to be the mental creator of anything durable.

The risk ensues that there will fade away from art that culture of the studios which is not only disciplinary but likewise gives works of art their intrinsic value; from science, that training in knowledge and research which is sustained by a sense of the whole; from philosophy, the faith that is handed down from person to person. There will be substituted for these the traditions of technical routine, of a merely manual dexterity, of form, of exact methods, and, lastly, of a futile talkativeness.

It is, therefore, the destiny of those who still endeavour to achieve originality to find that their powers are utterly paralysed; or at best what they produce is no more than fragmentary and unsuccessful. Few will be found competent to undertake what demands incredible capacity for enterprise and the faculty for pleasing the crowd.

Art. Architecture is the art which, in our epoch, secures the approval both of an élite and of the masses. The technical objectivity of engineering pursues an anonymous development, until the perfected and purposive forms for articles of daily use are discovered. The restrictions, here, to what is effectively controllable result in a perfectionment thanks to which the product of human skill seems to have a sort of natural necessity, so that there are no lacunæ, no harshnesses, no redundancies. But in technical objectivity as such, however perfect it may be, there is no style of the kind that prevailed in earlier times, none of that style which allowed a transcendental aim to peep through even in the most extravagant artifices of ornament and decoration. Our gratification with the self-evident and clear lines, spaces, and forms of technique is, therefore, rarely self-sufficient. Since our age has not yet discovered a style for itself or become fully aware what it really wants, the utilitarianism of purpose is dominant; and modern churches seem uncongenial because they have no adequate technical purpose. Furthermore, dissatisfaction involuntarily leads to disturbances of technical purity. In titanic examples, certainly, we note a success which is something greater than that of practical form, and which is analogous to style. Here it would seem that architects compete in unenvious rivalry, striving jointly to achieve something which they all regard as the fulfilment of sincerely performed tasks on behalf of the general life of contemporary man. Amid the hideous masquerade of European buildings there has become apparent of late years in public edifices, in town-planning, in machines and in the means of communication, in dwelling-houses and in pleasure-gardens, something which is not merely negatively simple and straightforward, but is endowed with a positively gratifying aspect and with a feeling for the environment. The creation of such things is more than the expression of a passing fashion, and has lasting value.

But instead of seeking to create articles of intrinsic worth by giving them an incalculable beauty of form in which the boldness of technical purity is overcome, the typical trend of our time is to proceed from objectivity towards its very opposite by having recourse to a succession of arbitrary changes. The sobriety of our technical world, wherein, though transcendentalism is lacking, machinery has been perfected, is continually crumbling away through an abandonment of this path of creative success on which only a small percentage of modern buildings are to be found. However, it seems probable that in respect of originality no other art can to-day vie with architecture.

In old days the plastic arts, music, and poesy were so germane to man in his totality that his transcendentalism was plainly manifest in them. Since the world through whose transfiguration art took shape has now been shattered, the question arises where the creative artist can discover the true being which, though now slumbering, can only emerge into consciousness and secure development through him. To-day it seems as if the arts were being whipped forward through life. There is no altar on which they can find rest or where their values can secure expression. Whereas in earlier decades impressionism was still instinct with the repose of contemplation, and whereas naturalism still effected the conquest of the present as material for possible artistic creation, it would seem that to-day, in the flux of events, the world had completely lost the faculty of creative repose. There now no longer prevails a feeling that the mind is the world of a community which could be reflected in art; we discern nothing but stupendous reality as a still speechless obscurity. In face of this it seems as if people could neither laugh nor weep, and even satire is dumb. The attempt to grasp reality naturalistically exceeds human power. To describe the torments of the individual, to effect a pregnant description of the peculiarities of the present, to record facts in a novel—these are certainly achievements, but they are not yet art.

To-day, as always, art must, willy-nilly, make transcendentalism perceptible, doing so at all times in the form which arouses contemporary faith. It may well be that the moment draws near when art will once again tell man what his God is and what he himself is. So long as we (as if this were not yet taking place) have to contemplate the tragedy of man, the sheen of true being, in the forms of a long-past world—not because the old art was a better art, but because as yet we have no truth of our own—though we do indeed participate in the genuine labours of our contemporaries as our situation, still we do it with the consciousness that we are failing to grasp our own world.

What is to-day obvious to all is a decay in the essence of art. Insofar as in the technical mass-order art becomes a function of this life, it approximates itself to sport as an object of pleasure. As pleasure, indeed, it frees itself from the coercion of the working life, but cannot further the selfhood of the individual. Instead of the objectivity of an emblem of the supra-sensual, it has only the objectivity of a concrete game. The search for a new attachment to form finds a discipline of form without the intrinsic value which could permeate the essence of man. Instead of effecting the liberation of the consciousness in contemplation of the being of transcendentalism, it becomes a renunciation of the possibility of selfhood in which transcendentalism can first disclose itself. The practice of art along these lines is, no doubt, something which demands marked ability; but essentially such art appeals to average impulses. The mass-man is presented to himself as furthering life in ways that are not regarded as questionable. Art of this kind voices the opposition to man's true nature as man, in favour of an immediate and crude present. Yearning for or delight in past greatness or any claim upon transcendentalism is represented as illusion. In all objectivity, form here becomes technique, construction becomes calculation, and aspiration a mere demand for the making of records. To the extent that art has lapsed into this function, it has become unprincipled. Changing from day to day, it may insist now on this now on that as essential; and everywhere it is in search of sensation. It necessarily lacks what used to be its unquestionable moral substance, the tie of intrinsic value. It is essentially chaotic, notwithstanding its display of objective ability. Life sees in it only its vitality or the negation thereof, and fashions for itself the illusion of another life, a romanticism of technique, an imagination of form, a superabundance

of enjoyment, adventure and crime, pleasurable non-
sense, and life which seems to overcome itself in
senseless daring.

For those who adopt this attitude towards art, the
theatre can become a mere place of entertainment, for
the gratification of curiosity and of the need for
illusion. Still, even so, a genuine tone is audible, or
perhaps I should call it an undertone which is easily
drowned.

The cinema discloses a world which would otherwise have remained unseen. We are fascinated by
the indiscreet revelation of the physiognomical reality
of human beings. Our optical experiences are
extended to all peoples and to all countries. But
what we are shown is not shown thoroughly or in a
way which enables us to dwell on the prospect. What
we see on the screen is stimulating, nay affecting, so
that we do not forget it; but most of the hours spent
in the picture theatre have to be paid for by a peculiar
and unexampled dreariness of mind which persists
when the tension of sightseeing has passed off.

Spectacular art still has a traditional technique. In
its newer development it can, for a moment, exert an
astonishingly powerful influence. A Piscator production, with its medley of machines, streets, dancing
legs, marching soldiers, presents us with a crude
reality which at the same time it lifts into a region of
unreality. When everything casts its shadows in a
calculated illumination, and is thus presented to us
twice over, seeming to live a second time as the ghost
of its first appearance, the technical mechanism as a
means of presentation seems to abolish the reality of
this mechanism. But, through this abolition, the
sense of being is lost; there remains only a nullity
which, in its appeal to the spectator, arouses a horror

of life. As a counteraction to this, the political trend is ineffective and no more than accessory.

The modern actor is able to give an elemental presentation of the primary affects of life: hatred, irony, and contempt; whorish eroticism, ludicrous figures; clamorous, simple, and convincing antitheses. In the vast majority of cases, however, he fails when he is called upon to show forth the nobility of man. Scarcely any one can now be found competent to impersonate Hamlet or Edgar.

Mozart's operas can still be admirably played to enthusiastic audiences, and indeed the best music of earlier days can be reproduced in a spirit of lofty aspiration, and without being degraded by adaptation to the instincts of the masses. We have no right to ask whether Piscator's public or Mozart's public is a better one, is more in touch with the truth. Here we are not concerned with alternatives, since we are dealing with incomparable entities. Piscator's public is one for which the chaos of the moment is being ephemerally brought into consciousness with a crude awareness of life as null; but in the reproduction of classical music we have art which makes true being vocal.

Music to-day is an art which appeals both to the multitude and to the élite. In contradistinction to architecture, however, it is likewise the most unrestrained in its reproduction of the past. This is the core of its effect. I refer, of course, to classical music. As far as modern music is concerned, this, in relation to the whole, is interesting rather than profoundly appealing, its peculiarities being those of attraction rather than those of fulfilment.

Science. Even to-day the sciences continue to achieve the most extraordinary results. The exact sciences, the natural sciences, have entered upon a phase of stimulating and rapid advance in respect of their fundamental notions and their empirical results. Scientific investigators throughout the world have formed relationships of rational mutual understanding. One passes the ball to another. This process has its repercussion among the masses in the ready comprehensibility of the results. In the mental and moral sciences, a vision that keeps close to facts has become microscopically keen. There has come into being an unprecedented abundance of documents and monuments. Critical security has been achieved.

Still, neither the tumultuous advance of the natural sciences nor yet the expansion of the field of the abstract sciences has been able to hinder the spread of increasing doubt concerning science in general. The natural sciences lack a comprehensive view. Despite the extent to which they have been unified, their basic notions are more of the nature of experimental recipes than truths which have been definitively conquered. The abstract sciences lack the sentiment of a humanist culture. It is true that they achieve valuable demonstration, but they are particularist and give the impression of being the perfectionment of a possibility which will perhaps lead no further. The upshot of the campaign of philological and critical research against a comprehensive view of the history of philosophy has been an incapacity to present history as the aggregate of human possibilities. The extension of historical lore into remoter millenniums, has doubtless resulted in objective discoveries, but has not led to any fresh appropriation of substantial humanhood. A dreary indifference would seem to be widely felt as regards all the past of our race.

But the crisis in which the sciences have become

involved does not relate so much to the limits of scientific capacity as to our sense of the significance of science in general. With the decay of a feeling for the whole and in view of the immeasurable extent of the knowable, the question has arisen whether the knowable is worth knowing. When knowledge is only considered valid apart from any comprehensive or all-embracing philosophy, it will be esteemed on account of its technical utility. It will lapse into the infinity of all those things which are really no one's concern. The causes of this crisis are in part dependent upon the course of science itself. Owing to the vastness of the acquisitions of science and to the refinement and multiplication of its methods, there has been a steady increase in the preliminary knowledge demanded of those who belong to each successive generation, before they become able to collaborate in scientific work. It might be thought that science has already exceeded the bounds of what a human being is able to grasp. Before he can master the domain of its previous conquests, death makes an end of him. But when science is pursued for some definite and unified purpose, its infinity can be disregarded, the student being content to master a special group of fundamental principles and outlooks. Ever since man began seriously to think, the extent of knowledge has exceeded the scope of any polyhistor. But from age to age the necessary insight has disclosed the means requisite for mastery. What science is, is realisable for the individual and the totality of the knowing man. At the present stage of our knowledge and capacity, therefore, the presuppositions handed down from the past represent, perhaps, a unique possibility which has not yet been grasped.

The fact that to-day the roots are perpetually being

questioned, that ultimate principles are being sought for and played off against one another, delivers over to doubt those who have no more than a half-knowledge. When firm foundations are lacking, what is known hangs in the air. Still, such a view of knowledge is taken only by those who do not participate in it. Doubtless the creative steps towards new principles make the edifice of acquired knowledge totter; but this becomes firmly established once more in the continuity of research which, though it has put the old acquisitions to the question, cherishes them under a new signification for the totality of the science concerned.

It is not, therefore, upon the immanent development of the sciences that the crisis really depends, but upon the human beings who are affected by the scientific situation. Not science *per se*, but man in the realm of science, is in a critical position. The historico-sociological cause of the crisis is to be found in the mass-life. The result of the transformation of the free research of individuals into the working enterprise of science at large has been that every one regards himself as able to collaborate, provided only he has understanding and diligence. There has arisen a sort of scientific plebeianism. People who wish to plume themselves as investigators draw empty analogies; they record any sort of data, make enumerations, pen descriptions, and tell us that they are contributing to empirical science. The endless multiplicity of outlooks (so that, in an increasing number of instances, those who are ostensibly working in the same branch of science fail to understand one another) arises from the fact that all sorts of irresponsible persons venture to formulate opinions which they have thrashed out for themselves and which they believe to convey a meaning. They are brazen-faced enough "to moot, merely as a topic for discussion," the first thoughts that come into their head. In the minds of the masses, the incredible superfluity of printed rationality becomes in many domains, and at last, no more than a demonstration of the chaos that prevails where there were at one time living thoughts, but are now only vestiges imperfectly understood. When "science" as thus conceived becomes a function of thousands of persons who are nothing but professional representatives of various interests, the result will be, owing to the qualities of the average man, that even the feeling for research and for literature will be lost. There are many sciences in which a literary sensation, a spurious journalism, will lead, temporarily, to a striking success. The result of all this is a conviction of the meaninglessness of science.

Where, in the domain of science, there persists the continuity of fruitful discovery, this has often been rendered possible only by the criterion of technical verification, for the reason that there is no longer any primary wish for knowledge driving the investigator towards his goal. In such cases the pecuniary rewards, which discoveries in the technical field will bring, serve to keep scientific research going despite the paralysis of its primary impetus. This renders possible a state of mind thanks to which, although the fault is purely subjective, an objective crisis is supposed to exist. The process of the mental self-evacuation of science is continued in favour of the mechanised life of the masses, thanks to the offer of rewards which enable competent intelligences to devote themselves to the work of purposive discovery even though they have no love of science for its own sake.

Mass-life at the universities tends to destroy science

as science. Science must adapt itself to the crowd, who care for it only on account of its immediate practical results, who learn merely in order to pass an examination and acquire the status which success in this matter gives them. Research is only to be promoted insofar as it can promise practically utilisable results. "Science", as thus understood, has become nothing more than the rational objectivity of the learnable. What used to be a university wherein the lively mental atmosphere of *sapere aude* prevailed, has degenerated to become no more than a school. An enforced curriculum relieves the individual from the risks attendant upon seeking a path for himself. But without the hazards of liberty, there can be no possibility of independent thought. The final result is the skill of the specialised technician, and perhaps comprehensive knowledge—the pundit, not the investigator, being the prevalent type. As a symptom of the decay of science we have the fact that people are now ceasing to draw any distinction between the two.

True science is the aristocratic affair of those who select themselves for its pursuit. The primary will to know, which nothing but a crisis of the sciences could render impossible, is entertained by the individual at his own peril. Doubtless, nowadays, there is something abnormal about any one who devotes his whole life to research; but, after all, there have never been multitudes willing to do so. Even he who uses science for the practical ends of this or that profession, is only a participator in science if by temperament, and in his inner man, he is an investigator. The crisis of the sciences is a crisis of the individuals who are affected thereby because, although they are "scientific workers", they have not been inspired by a genuine and absolute will to know.

An erroneous understanding of the significance of science is, therefore, widespread to-day throughout the world. At one time science was regarded with remarkable respect. Since the mass-order is only rendered possible by technique, and technique is only rendered possible by science, there is, even in our epoch, a general faith in science. But inasmuch as science only becomes accessible through methodical culture, and since astonishment at the achievements of science does not imply participation in its significance, this faith is no more than superstition. Genuine science is a knowledge that is accompanied by knowledge of the methods and limits of knowledge. But if there be a faith in the results of science for their own sake, regardless of the way in which they are acquired, the superstition thus engendered becomes a substitute for genuine faith. People cling to the reputed solidity of scientific data. The contents of that superstition are: a utopian expertise concerning all that can further production, and the technical mastery of every difficulty in this field; welfare as the possibility of the life of the community at large, as the possibility of democracy as the right path towards liberty for all through majority rule;-and, in general, a faith in the data of the understanding regarded as dogmas unquestionably valid. Almost every one is under the spell of this superstition, men of learning not excepted. In individual instances it will seem to have been overcome, and yet even then it will continually recur. An abyss yawns, on the one hand, between those who fall a prey to it, and, on the other, the critical reason of genuine science.

Scientific superstition is very readily transformed into hostility to science, into a superstitious faith in the help supposed to be derivable from powers which negate science. One who, having faith in the omnipotence of science, has suppressed his own thoughts, when confronted with the expert, is apt, should this expert prove a broken reed, to turn away in his disillusionment and put his trust in a charlatan. A faith in science that has degenerated into superstition is closely akin to humbug.

Anti-scientific superstition, in its turn, will masquerade as science, proclaiming "a true science which has superseded the science of the doctrinaires". The mentality of our generation has been clouded by astrology, Christian Science, theosophy, spiritualism, clairvoyance, occultism, and the like. Anti-science stalks abroad to-day amid all parties and sects and manifests its influence among persons of the most diversified outlooks, pulverising the very substance of rational human existence. It is a sign of the decay of selfhood that so few persons are able to remain genuinely scientific even in the sphere of practical thought. Effective intercommunication of minds becomes impossible amid the nebulosity of this superstition, which destroys the possibility alike of genuine knowledge and genuine scientific faith.

Philosophy. The situation of philosophy is to-day characterised by three indefinite realities. First of all, the epoch has produced a vast number of persons devoid of all faith and receiving their stamp exclusively from the apparatus. Secondly religion, though represented admirably enough by ecclesiastical organisations, would seem to have lost the power of creative expression in conformity with an actual present. In the third place philosophy has, during a whole century, become, it would appear, more and more a mere enterprise of doctrine and history, thus increasingly renouncing its true function.

The general loss of faith is, as it were, an indictment of the world of technical apparatus. The wonderful advances made by man, the advances thanks to which he has been enabled in great measure to control nature and to mould the material world in forms suited to his own purposes, have been accompanied, not only by an enormous increase in population, but also by the spiritual atrophy of innumerable persons whom no one can hold responsible for the reality of the origin and the course of their lives. Yet when we ask if men in the vast majority are to wither in the service of the apparatus, we realise that the only possible road is that along which we have to proceed in conjunction with the apparatus and to strive for rescue even while we are enmeshed in it. Still, the man without faith does not become a mere beast of burden, but remains a human being. For that very reason, as he himself perceives, everything has become opaque to him. All that is left active in him is the blind will to change the conditions and to change himself. His eagerness to do so increases, for man is incapable of living without faith. In the world of unfaith there are many who still retain the possibility of faith, but these are stifled in the germ when there is no tradition and when every one is thrust back upon himself. However, no plan and no organisation can render possible that which ultimately none can achieve except by his own activities, as man realising the full possibility of human existence.

In the sanctimoniousness which the consciousness of technique and of man's life engenders as the consciousness of the production of all things, the true inwardness of the indubitably unconditioned is lost. Religion as the historical basis of human existence has become, so to say, invisible. Religion, indeed, persists, administered by the Churches and the creeds;

but in the mass-life it is often nothing more than consolation in time of trouble or than an orderly conduct of life, being rarely now persistent as an effective vital energy. Although the Church retains its efficiency as a political power, religious faith actively held by individuals grows continually rarer. Nowadays the great traditions of the Churches have often become nothing more than a futile attempt to restore their irrevocable past, side by side with a broad-minded adoption of all kinds of modern thought. Yet it grows continually harder for the Church to tolerate individual independence. It no longer embodies the genuine tension of authority and freedom; but is able on the other hand, by the ruthless expulsion of those who think for themselves, to achieve a remarkable concentration of its mental apparatus for the control of the mass-mind.

For centuries philosophic thought had sustained a consciousness of the ultimate reason of human existence, had secularised religion, and had decisively realised the independence of the free individual. The individual did not lose his foundation, for, in its absolute historicity, this was but more brightly illuminated. The reality of the individual only remained questionable because the illumination could fade and become vacant in an unalloyed consciousness without existence. In fact, from the opening of the second half of the nineteenth century the traditional philosophy became everywhere an enterprise carried on by university schools which more and more seldom were communities of philosophic persons drawing from their own sources and communicating in the form of thought what had welled up in their own consciousness. Philosophy was divorced from its origin, and had no longer any responsibility for the real life it rendered possible as the doctrine of a secondary phenomenon. It tried to justify itself as against the sciences (whose superiority it actually recognised) by giving itself out to be pure science and in the belief that under the name of epistemology it could establish the validity and the significance of the sciences as well as its own. For all its apparent contemporaneousness it became in fact identical with a knowledge of its own history. But even this was, for the most part, not so much an assimilation of the origin of philosophy as an obsession with fragments of doctrine, with problems, with opinions, and with systems. Outwardly learned, inwardly rationalistic, devoid of any relationship with the life of the individual, it still, thanks to its tradition of strictly logical thought, was able to carry on the serviceable enterprise of the philosophical schools which, despite the violently polemical atmosphere of their literature, were all fundamentally identical, although they bore various names, such as idealism, positivism, neo-Kantianism, criticism, phenomenology, objectivity. The most characteristic symptom of the philosophical weakness of these multifariously named philosophical schools is that most of their exponents knew nothing of Kierkegaard; that they did not accept Nietzsche as a philosopher but classified him as an imaginative writer or a poet, and thus "drew his teeth and pared his claws"; that they made light of Nietzsche as unscientific, as one of the crazes of the moment, as an incapable. They watered down the radical problem of philosophy until it could no longer be dangerous.

Philosophy, thus renouncing its task, multiplied its enterprises but reduced itself to chaos. The task it renounced was sublime. Only through philosophy could man, being no longer able to guide his life in accordance with the dictates of a revealed religion, become aware of his own true will. He, indeed, who is loyal to transcendentalism in the form of such a revealed faith, should never be attacked so long as he does not grow intolerant; for to attack the faith of a believer is purely destructive. Perhaps the believer may be open to philosophical argument and may venture to entertain that doubt which is inseparable from human life; but he still retains as outlet and standard the positiveness of being in historical form, and he therefore returns inevitably to his own way of thinking. With this possibility we have now no concern. To-day unfaith is a mighty current apposite to the time. It is questionable whether faith is possible without religion. Philosophy originates in this question. The significance of philosophising to-day is our attempt to confirm ourselves in a faith that arises independently of revelation. Bruno, Spinoza, and Kant were forerunners, were pioneers, in this field. When religion has been lost (I consider that religion exists only under the ægis of ecclesiasticism, and that to speak of religion in any other sense is a compromising deception), there may remain either the fantasies and the fanaticisms of superstition, or else philosophy. All this is faith only in and through self-understanding. Reflective philosophy wants to clarify it systematically, and to give a connected account of what really can only rise fully into consciousness in existence, and not in a thought-process which is continually tending to break away from existence. The fantasies of superstition need no philosophy; they can dispense with ecclesiastico-religious security, but they, too, try to find sanction of some sort; whilst ecclesiastical faith needs nothing but theology to sustain its communal life. Philosophy, however, is on the side of the individual as an individual, that is to say it hoists the banner of liberty—whether it does so as an audacious venture and pretentiously, or, maybe, as the illusion of a poor wretch who is in truth God-forsaken and can find no salvation outside the Church.

To-day philosophy is the only refuge for those who, in full awareness, have no safe standing-ground in religion. No longer is it the affair of a restricted circle, of an élite; for, at any rate as the individual's urgent question how he can best live, it has become the affair of countless numbers of persons. The philosophy of the schools was justified insofar as it rendered a philosophical life possible. To-day, however, it is incomplete, discursive, disintegrated and disintegrating.

These considerations explain to us the origin of the seductive call, the sirens' voice, which for so long now has been making itself heard: "Back from consciousness to the unconsciousness of the blood, of faith, of the earth; back from the spirit, the historical, and the unquestionable." Religion was despairingly exaggerated into absurdities, because it was no longer believed with a primary faith. Though they had really lost faith, people wanted to force themselves to believe by stifling their consciousness.

This call is deceptive. Man, if he is to remain man, must advance by way of consciousness. There is no road leading backward. Crude consciousness, whereby everything is represented as cognisable knowledge and as obvious purpose, is to be overcome by philosophy through a lucid development of all the modes of consciousness. We can no longer veil reality from ourselves by renouncing self-consciousness without simultaneously excluding ourselves from the historical course of human existence. In life, self-consciousness has become the condition under which the genuine unassailably emerges, the unconditioned can establish itself firmly, and our identity with our own historicity becomes possible.

Philosophy has become the foundation of man's true being. To-day it is assuming its characteristic form. Man, torn from the sheltering substantiality of stable conditions and cast into the apparatus of mass-life, deprived of his faith by the loss of his religion, is devoting more decisive thought to the nature of his own being. Thus it is that there have arisen the typical philosophical ideas adequate to our own epoch. No longer does the revealed Deity upon whom all is dependent come first, and no longer the world that exists around us; what comes first is man, who, however, cannot make terms with himself as being, but strives to transcend himself.

PART FOUR

OUR PRESENT CONCEPTION OF HUMAN EXISTENCE

THE insecure human being gives our epoch its physiognomy: in rebelliousness; in the despair of nihilism; in the perplexity of the multitude of persons who remain unfulfilled; in a search along false paths on the part of those who renounce finite goals and withstand harmonising lures. "There is no God," cry the masses more and more vociferously; and with the loss of his God man loses his sense of values—is, as it were, massacred because he feels himself of no account.

The aspect of our world in the coercion of its life and in the instability of its mental activity renders it impossible for being to retain a satisfactory grip upon the extant. Our representation of the outer world tends to discourage us. We have a pessimistic outlook; we incline to renounce action. In other cases, however, despite our gloomy picture of the world in general, we preserve an indolently optimistic consciousness of our own personal joy in life and are satisfied with our contemplation of the substantial—for such an attitude is to-day common enough. But pessimism and optimism are both over-simplifications, and are the outcome of a shirking of the situation.

In actual fact, however, the demands which the situation makes upon man are so exacting that none but a being who should be something more than man would seem capable of complying with them. The impossibility of complying with these demands leads us to evade them, to accommodate ourselves to that which is transitorily present, and to arrest our thoughts at a boundary. One who believes that everything is in order and who trusts in the world as it now is, does not even need to be equipped with courage. He complies with the course of events which (so he believes) work for good without his participation. His alleged courage is nothing more than a confidence that man is not slipping down into an abyss. One who truly has courage is one who, inspired by an anxious feeling of the possible, reaches out for the knowledge that he alone who aims at the impossible can attain the possible. Only through experience of the impossibility of achieving fulfilment does man become enabled to perform his allotted task.

Contemporary man does not receive his imprint simply from the fact that he appropriates what comes to him as being out of the tradition of his world. If he gives himself up to this tradition alone, he is at a loose end. He is, in a new sense, dependent upon himself as an individual. He must help himself, seeing that he can no longer attain freedom by assimilation of the all-permeating substance, but is at rest in the void of the null. When the transcendental conceals itself, man can attain to it only through his own self.

If man is to help himself, his philosophy, to-day, must take the form of a study of what is our present conception of human existence. The old antitheses—the contrasted outlooks known respectively as individualism and socialism, liberal and conservative, revolutionary and reactionary, progressive and reversionary, materialistic and idealistic—are no longer valid, although they are still universally flaunted as banners or used as invectives. An accommodation to various philosophies, as if there were various philosophies among which it was necessary to choose, is no longer the way of attaining to truth. An expansion of vision and cognition to all that is possible has culminated to-day in the unrestraint in which there is an untransferable choice between the null, on the one hand, and, on the other, the absolute historicity of one's own foundation, which is at one with the consciousness of an obligatory limit.

But the problem of human existence, the solution of which is to lead us out of the dogmatism of the objectivity of fixed alternative philosophies, is not, as such, by any means unambiguous.

Man is always something more than what he knows of himself. He is not what he is simply once for all, but is a process; he is not merely an extant life, but is, within that life, endowed with possibilities through the freedom he possesses to make of himself what he will by the activities on which he decides.

Man is not a finished life which repeats itself from generation to generation, nor is he a manifest life which plainly reveals itself to him. He "makes good" in virtue of the passivity of perpetually renewed identical circles, and is dependent upon his own activity, whereby the process of his life is carried on towards an unknown goal.

Consequently there is a profound cleavage in man's innermost nature. Whatever he thinks of himself, he must think against himself and against what is not-himself. He sees everything in conflict or in contradiction.

The significance of his outlook varies according as he sunders himself into spirit and flesh, into understanding and sensuality, into soul and body, into duty and inclination—also into his being and its phenomenal aspect, into his actions and his thoughts, into what he actually does and what he thinks he is doing. The decisive point is that he must always be setting himself in opposition to himself. There is no human existence without cleavage. Yet he cannot rest content in this cleavage. The way in which he overcomes it, the way in which he transcends it, reveals the conception he has of himself.

In that respect we find that there are two alternatives, which must be adequately discussed.

Man may make himself the object of cognition. He then regards as his true being what, in daily experience, he recognises as his life and its underlying ground. What he phenomenally is, is his consciousness; and his consciousness is what it is in virtue of something else, in virtue of the sociological circumstances, in virtue of the unconscious, in virtue of the vital form. This not-himself is for him being, whose essence is reflected for him phenomenally as consciousness.

The significance of this mode of cognition is that contention is overcome through being becoming identical with consciousness. The idea of mere life as completed in a condition wherein there are no tensions is, in this mode of cognition, involuntarily regarded as attainable. There is deemed possible a sociological order wherein all will enter into their rights; a mind wherein the unconscious and the conscious will be amicable companions as soon as the former has been purged of all its complexes; a racial vitality which, after an efficient process of artificial selection has done its work, will lead to the universalisation of a healthy mind and body so that all will be satisfied in a perfected life. In these circumstances which (in an ambiguous sense) are regarded as both necessary and true, there will no longer be any unconditionality of temporal life, for unconditionality arises only out of the tensions that affect self-existence. Such a mode of cognition, which is characteristic of a natural human existence, revolts against selfhood or self-existence as against something forlorn, self-exclusive, morbid, and extravagant.

But it is the course against which natural human existence revolts which is the course taken by the second possibility. Here man finds himself to be the subject of tensions regarded as definitively the outcome of limitary situations that are inevitable in life, these becoming manifest with the peremptoriness of selfhood. If man be no longer recognised as being (which he is), then he finds himself cognitively in the suspense of absolute possibility. Therein he experiences the appeal to his freedom, in virtue of which he is able to become what it is possible for him to become but what he is not as yet. As freedom he conjures up being as his latent transcendentalism.

The significance of this path is transcendentalism. Mere life miscarries. From this outlook, the search for a complete freedom from tensions is seen to be an illusion wherein people falsely suppose themselves to have escaped from the limitary situation and to have overcome time. All cognition in the world, human cognition included, is a particular perspective by means of which man finds the scope of his situation. Cognition is, therefore, in the hands of the man who can outstep it. But he himself is incomplete and insusceptible of completion, delivered over to something other than himself. By thought he can do nothing more than throw light upon his path.

Inasmuch as man, in all his cognitions, still does not discover himself to be thoroughly known, and therefore incorporates his circumstantial knowledge into his philosophical process, he once more secures expression, this time through himself. That which he had lost when he was wholly thrust back upon himself, may now become once more manifest to him in a new form. Only during a fallacious moment of despair concerning crude life did he consider himself identical, as knower, with the origin of all. When he proceeds to contemplate himself seriously, he becomes once more aware of that which is something more than himself. In the world he grasps anew the objectivity which had threatened to become petrified in indifference or to be lost in subjectivity; in transcendentalism he grasps the being which, in his own freedom as phenomenal life, he had mistaken for self-existence.

These two possibilities are to-day current as doctrines under well-known names; they are expounded in a confused manner, for they have not yet acquired any definitively valid form, but they are an almost inseparable part of the terminology of contemporary man.

The cognitions of human existence which are to be grasped in particular trends have become, as sociology, psychology, and anthropology, the typical modern sciences which, when they put forward a claim to absolute validity and pretend themselves to be capable of cognising man's being as a whole, must be rejected as utterly inadequate substitutes for philosophy. A valid philosophy arises only out of that revolutionary change in the way of contemplating human existence which is known to-day as existence-philosophy. This latter finds the material of its terminology in the domains which, as a knowledge of man, are simultaneously bounded and safeguarded by it. But it transcends them in its approximation towards being itself. Existence-philosophy is the philosophy of human existence which once more transcends man.

1. THE SCIENCES OF MANKIND

Sociology. Since man only exists in and through society, to which he owes life, tradition, and the duties that are incumbent on him, we must study his nature by studying society. The individual human being seems incomprehensible, but society is not. Instead of studying man as an individual, we must study the social institutions of mankind, and these will lead us to a knowledge of man's being. Social corporations, the forms of civilisation, mankind at large, are the aspects of human existence. The science of them is known as sociology, and of this science there are manifold varieties.

For example, the Marxians believe themselves scientifically enabled to grasp the true being of man. Man, they say, is the outcome of his life as a social being, contemplated as the mode in which the necessaries of life are produced. In his peculiarities, he is himself a product of the place he occupies in society. His consciousness is a function of his sociological situation. His mentality is no more than a super-structure erected upon the foundation of the material realities of an extant way of supplying the necessaries of human life. Philosophies are but ideologies which have come into being in order to justify the particular interests that dominate in a typical situation. Those

173

who share such interests dominant in a particular situation constitute a class. Classes change in accordance with changes in the means of production. To-day there are two classes, that of the workers and that of the capitalists. The State is an instrument of class dominion, the means whereby one of these classes keeps the other class in a state of subordination. Religion is "the opium of the people"; it is something with which the members of the subordinate class are doped, are kept in a condition of contented dependence. But this outcome of class opposition is only inevitable during a transient phase in the development of the means of production. When that phase has been surpassed, there will arise a classless society wherein there will be no ideologies and therefore no religion (for religion is but one of the various ideologies), no State, and therefore no exploitation; but mankind will exist as a unified society which, with perfect justice and full scope for freedom, will see to it that the needs of all are supplied. During the present phase of history man is advancing towards this goal, which will inevitably be reached through the active exercise of the will of a majority—although at the moment those who actively will the attainment of the goal are no more than a minority which constitutes the vanguard of the march towards a better future. Man, having grasped the nature of his own being, can henceforward plan out his development, and can accelerate the coming of what is in any case necessary. His being and his consciousness are no longer sundered, but are becoming unified. Without knowing it, man has been dependent upon the things which he produces. Now he will become their master; for deliberately, wittingly, having attained to a scientific knowledge of the inevitable course of his development,

he will take over the whole conduct of his own life.
Devotion to State or Church is superseded. Man,
grasping the nature of his own being, devotes himself
to the class which will bring into existence a free,
classless society—devotes himself to the proletariat.

This whole outlook, however, far from being a
scientific cognition, is nothing more than an intellectualist faith which, confronted by the question
whether it be not itself the mere ideology of a class,
can maintain itself only by the blind mental brutality
of such a mode of belief. From it proceeds, when
faith is paralysed, the conception which animates
those who, at the outset, regard every possible position
as an ideology because they start from presuppositions
which are not truly valid. Everything, they say, is
relative, and nothing is self-existent beyond material
interests and the impulses of human beings. In truth
such a sociology effects no cognitions, but merely
gives expression to a faith in the null by affixing its
own labels to everything that happens.

Marxism is the best known and most familiar
example of sociological analyses. By investigations
of the kind, particular and relative cognitions are
achieved; but simultaneously they are expressions of
a mental struggle on behalf of the modes of human
existence. Common to them all, therefore, is the
contention that being is absolute. The arguments
whereby they are sustained upon the basis of such
mutable presuppositions are changeable at will and
can be played off one against the other. In this
reputed knowledge, man as he truly is always goes
astray.

The decisive step, that which first establishes knowledge as knowledge and therefore liberates man, is
taken when the significance of an objective cognition

of the manifestation of will is not merely sharply distinguished in theory from the contemporary historical situation, but also remains the goal of radical activity in life itself. In our own time this step was taken by Max Weber.

For him sociology is no longer the philosophy of human existence. It is the particular science of human behaviour and its consequences. He regards the cognisable relationship as relative. He knows that, in the infinite complications of historical reality, the effective influence of any particular causal factor lies outside the range of possible calculation; and he is aware that the image of a whole can be nothing more than one aspect in circumstantial contemplation, and cannot be a knowledge of the real whole. This relativist cognition leaves man in himself untouched. It is man as such for whom the various modes of insight become possibilities and limits; he grasps the cognisability of his situation in life, but he does not lift himself up into the known and the knowable. This attitude of mind demands that the possible insights, in their relativity, should become an actual possession, and should be immediately present when something is being done responsibly; but it rejects the idea that such responsibility should be shuffled off upon a dogmatic knowledge considered to be endowed with objective accuracy, and it demands that the dangers and the hazards of genuine activity in the world should be accepted.

Psychology. In former days, psychology was a part of, a building-stone in, the thought-out edifice of life. Working constructively with the aid of metaphysical principles, it gave a diagram of the elements and the forces of the mind, illustrating this by everyday observations or by the recounting of remarkable occurrences. During the nineteenth century, it became an aggregate of sensory and psychological data, loosely associated by theories of a subjacent unconscious. Entangled in a multitude of indifferent matters of infinitesimal importance, and tending more and more as a mere experimental enterprise to occupy itself about nullities, it became, in the end, nothing more than the embryo of a science. Kierkegaard and Nietzsche had revealed to it new depths as the vehicle of thought on the plane of existence-philosophy. Empirical discoveries of an entirely unanticipated kind were superadded from the domain of animal psychology and psychopathology. Novels and the drama were dominated by a psychological interpretation of everything.

Amid the medley of doctrines and facts, philosophical impulse and objective research, descriptions of the stream of consciousness and speculations regarding the unconscious, of psychology without a mind, and of cobwebs of the brain, there did not manifest himself any investigator able to resolve these tangles and to bring the knowable into harmony by a study of its inward interconnexion or by a methodical restriction of its domain to empirical, objectively cogent, and relative insight.

At length psychology became the general property of the epoch in a form that is extremely characteristic of our day, namely as the psychoanalysis founded by Sigmund Freud. But although this has the merit of drawing attention to previously unnoticed facts in the domain of psychopathology, it has also the defect that it has failed to make these facts unexceptionably appreciable; for, despite the vast extent of psycho-analytical literature, psychoanalysis still lacks an adequate and convincing record of cases. It restricts itself to the field of the plausible, of that which may temporarily seem impressive, but of which the significance cannot be fathomed by unscientific persons.

Psychoanalysis collects and interprets dreams, slips and blunders, involuntary associations, that it may in this way plumb the depths of the unconscious whereby the conscious life is determined. Man is the puppet of his unconscious, and when the latter has had a clear light thrown into it, he will become master of himself. In the unconscious are the basic impulses which are comprehended under the term *libido*, regarded, above all, as erotic impulse. The will to power, the self-assertive impulse, and, finally, a death-impulse, must be superadded. Such are the teachings of the psychoanalysts. But their doctrine is never unified, not even heuristically for a brief space, in order to advance from a clear statement of a problem into the realm of effective investigation. The psycho-analysts even plume themselves on being empiricists, that, year after year, while presenting an infinite quantity of material, they may go on reiterating what is fundamentally the same thing. The self-examination of a sincere thinker, which after the long-lasting Christian interlude attained its climax in Kierkegaard and Nietzsche, is in psychoanalysis degraded into the discovery of sexual longings and typical experiences of childhood; it is the masking of genuine but hazardous self-examination by the mere rediscovery of familiar types in a realm of reputed necessity wherein the lower levels of human life are regarded as having an absolute validity.

Thus in psychoanalysis there are gathered together various elements intended to show the perplexed masses what man really is. The instinct towards the affirmation of man in his all-too-human aspects finds an unintended gratification. The doctrine is used for the self-justification of life as it is, the *libido* and the other instincts or impulses being regarded as the true realities, just as material interests are by the Marxists regarded as the true realities. They are real enough, of course, but we have to set bounds to them, and to learn to contemplate human existence as something different from them. The tacit but logical outcome of psychoanalysis is to make felt (but not to think out) an ideal in which, from the cleavage and the coercion through which man could come to himself, he is to return to that nature in which he no longer needs to be man.

Anthropology. Anthropology relates to visible man in his original essence. It does not aim at a universally human psychology, but at a typical being of man as that which is simultaneously specific in the individual character. Anthropology is one of the means for comprehending the unique in its vitality as physique, race, character, the spirit of civilisation.

As against an idealism which would merely contemplate an imaginary spirit devoid of reality, and as against the materialist interpretation of history which would reduce man to nothing but a function, the anthropologists believe themselves able to discern man's true being.

Anthropology thus conceived is an aggregate held together by the fundamental notion of race. Physical anthropology studies the body, its structure and its functions, in the various species of man now actually diffused over the earth's surface. The anthropologist takes precise measurements of numerous human beings, and effects other observations of their aspect. But as far as knowledge of the being of man is concerned, his bodily characteristics are only relevant

179

when they are regarded as the physiognomical expression of his essence. An understanding of expression is the true source of anthropology insofar as it is concerned with human existence. Proceeding from physiognomy and the study of gesture by way of graphology to the morphology of civilisation, there becomes established a methodistically analogous attitude, that of an intuitively comprehending vision of the being which is articulated in the objectivity of the bodily form, of the movements that have been petrified in handwriting, of the work and the modes of action of individual human beings and of nations.

In the works (many of them notable works) wherein this anthropological vision has become concrete, we find such a medley of cogent objective knowledge and of intuitively expressionist understanding, that the validity of the former suggests to the reader the validity of the latter. Measurement after measurement is taken; but what is really seen eludes all measurement and the possibility of numerical statement. Information is imparted, but lacks a significance substantially identical with the alleged facts. For expressionist vision does not become cogent knowledge but remains a possibility merely, and is once more itself an expression for the essence of him who thus contemplates things. To him there appears in expression, not only the natural datum, but also the being of freedom.

The anthropological outlook incorporates the possibilities of spiritual vision, but promptly thereafter that which has been grasped by this spiritual vision undergoes degradation to a naturalistic being. Anthropological thought is dominated by the standard of vital duration, by the categories of growth and mortality; its involuntary presupposition is that we are competent to foster, to breed, nay to produce human beings and to grasp them in their entirety. To the anthropologist the multiplicity of the races of man is not an existential phenomenon in its historicity and destiny.

The impetus to this anthropology is not derived from a desire to justify average ordinariness. On the contrary, the anthropologist is impelled to his researches by a love for a noble and a hatred for an ignoble image of mankind. Thus there arise aspects of human beings as exemplars, and the counterparts of these. There arise in the mind, types towards which we would fain advance or which we would gladly avoid becoming. National types, occupational types, bodily types, are objectively distinguished, but in such a way that the distinction is at every moment animated by a secret love or aversion.

Another impulse is that towards self-knowledge in the realm of the possible. One sees oneself from a new outlook, and becomes insatiable in one's contemplation of one's fellow human beings. Occupation, parties, nations are disregarded, that man at an immense distance from man may be brought into the closest touch. One comes to recognise a kinship which is then objectified in images of a lofty kind.

But this procedure, which seemed on the way to become existence-philosophy, is separated from it by a vast chasm if it is rendered absolute to become a cognition of being. For implicit in it is an impulse to depreciate one's own being; the being of liberty being degraded to a mere given being which is tantamount to that of race. An inclination to regard oneself as nobler *qua* being, or, because one is less noble, to renounce one's claims, paralyses freedom by involving it in a naturalistic necessity.

In our study of sociology, psychology, and anthropology, we have been content to draw attention to a particular example of each. For Marxism, psychoanalysis, and ethnological theory are to-day the most widely diffused veilings of mankind. The direct brutality of hatred and of eulogy which have come to prevail with the development of mass-life finds its expression therein: in Marxism, the manner in which the masses want community life; in psychoanalysis, the way in which the masses seek a mere life-gratification; in ethnological theory, the fashion in which the masses would like to be better than others.

There are truths in all these doctrines, but they have not, so far, been expounded in all their possible purity. Who escaped, at one time, being fascinated by the *Communist Manifesto*, which gave a new glimpse into the possible causal interrelationships between economics and society? Every psychopathologist knows that he was given new glimpses of the truth by means of psychoanalysis. What is not encountered as an effective concept in ethnological theory, will probably in due course become something which will play a decisive part in the future of all mankind; but what this is and how it will come about, what possibilities are involved, is not yet plain. The most relevant are the particular insights that have been evolved from Marxism.

Without sociology, no sound political effort is possible. Without psychology, no one can ever succeed in mastering the confusion that prevails in his intercourse with himself and with others. Without anthropology, we lack an awareness of our own obscure foundations.

In any case, the range of cognition is restricted. No sociology can tell me what I will as destiny; no psychology can make it clear to me what I really am; the true being of man cannot be bred as a race. In all directions we reach the limit of what can be planned and made.

Cognitions are, indeed, material with which we can work in order to favour the desired course of life. But man is only sincere when he is able to distinguish genuine cognitions from mere possibilities. The theory of the dictatorship of the proletariat, the psychotherapeutic prescriptions of the psychoanalyst, the eugenist's notions concerning the possibility of breeding supermen, are, in view of the vagueness of their respective content, no more than brutalising demands which, at the very outset of attempts to realise them, would have effects utterly different from those desired by their advocates.

For Marxism, psychoanalysis, and ethnological theory (eugenics) have peculiarly destructive qualities! Just as Marxism assumes all spiritual life to be no more than a superstructure erected upon material foundations, so does psychoanalysis believe itself able to disclose this same spiritual life as the sublimation of repressed impulses; and what, by these lights, is still spoken of as civilisation or culture, is constructed like an obsessional neurosis. Ethnological theory (eugenics) entails a conception of history which is utterly hopeless. A negative selection of the best would soon lead to the ruin of true human existence; or else, owing to the essential characteristics of human nature, although by this process of racial intermingling great possibilities might be developed, at the end of the intermixture and within a few centuries an etiolated average life would have been brought into being to perpetuate itself for an indefinite period.

All these three trends incline to destroy what has been of worth to man. Above all they are ruinous to whatever is unconditioned, since, as knowledge, they parade as a false unconditioned which cognises everything else as conditioned. Not only must the Godhead be dethroned, but likewise every kind of philosophical faith. The most sublime and the meanest are dressed up in the same terminology that, tried and found wanting, they may be driven forth into the null.

The three trends in question are in conformity with the general mood of our time. What exists must be destroyed, either in order to leave room for the growth of an unknown novelty, or else that not a wrack may be left behind. For them the new is the rule of the intellect. Communism in one way, Freudism in another, and eugenics in a third, are unquestionably marching towards an ideal—but it is towards a future in which understanding and reality will be held valid in place of illusion and divinity. They will turn against any one who has faith, of whatever kind; and they will "unveil" him in their sense of the term. They offer no proofs, but merely reiterate comparatively simple methods of interpretation. They are irrefutable insofar as they themselves are the expression of a faith; they have faith in the null, and, in their faith, are fanatically confident in the dogmatism with which they cling to the forms of being that for them mask the null.—"There are only two classes, the bourgeoisie and the proletariat."—"These impulses or instincts and their modifications."—"These races." —The individual advocate of these theories may in reality hold an entirely different faith and may merely fail to understand himself.

2. EXISTENCE-PHILOSOPHY

Sociology, psychology, and anthropology teach that man is to be regarded as an object concerning which experiences are to be assembled, and that with the aid of these it will be possible to modify man through the working of institutions. This implies the recognition in man of something which is not man himself; yet man, as a possibility of a creature endowed with spontaneity, rises in revolt against being regarded as a mere result. What the individual can be transformed into sociologically or psychologically or anthropologically, is not accepted by him as cogent without qualification. By comprehending cognisable reality as something particular and relative, he emancipates himself from that which the sciences would like definitively to make of him. He perceives that the transgression of the limits of the cognisable by way of a dogmatic self-assertion of known being is nothing more than a deceptive substitute for true philosophy, and that those who wish to escape from freedom try to justify a spurious knowledge of being.

For his activities in every situation and in all occupations, man needs a specific expertise concerning things and concerning himself as life. But expertise is nowhere adequate *per se*, for it first becomes significant in virtue of him who possesses it. The use I make of it is primarily determined by my own will. The best laws, the most admirable institutions, the most trustworthy acquirements of knowledge, the most effective technique, can be used in conflicting ways. They are of no avail unless individual human beings fulfil them with an effective and valuable reality. What actually happens, therefore, cannot be modified by an improvement in expertise, but is exclusively decided by the being of man. Decisive is a man's inward attitude, the way in which he contemplates his world and grows aware of it, the essential value of his satisfactions—these things are the origin of what he does.

Existence-philosophy is the thought, making use of or transcending all expertise, by means of which man would fain become himself. This thought does not cognise objects, but illuminates and elaborates the being of the thinker. Brought into a state of suspense by having transcended the cognitions of the world (as the adoption of a philosophical attitude towards the world) that fixate being, it appeals to its own freedom (as the illumination of existence) and gains space for its own unconditioned activity through conjuring up transcendentalism (as metaphysics).

This existence-philosophy cannot be rounded off in any particular work, nor can it acquire definitive perfectionment as the life of any particular thinker. It was, in modern times, originated by Kierkegaard, and through him procured widespread diffusion. During his lifetime he had created a sensation in Copenhagen, but thereafter had passed into oblivion. Shortly before the Great War, people began to talk about him once more, but his period of effective influence has only just begun. Schelling, in the later development of his philosophical thought, entered paths on which, existentially, he made a breach in German idealism. But just as Kierkegaard sought vainly for a method of communication, and had to help himself out with the technique of pseudonyms and of his "psychological experimentation", so did Schelling bury his sound impulses and views in the idealistic systematisation which, having developed it in his youth, he was unable to rid himself of. Whereas Kierkegaard deliberately evaded the profoundest problem of philosophy, that of communication, and, in the desire to achieve an indirect communication, arrived at extraordinarily defective results, which nevertheless stimulated his readers—Schelling hardly became aware of what he was driving at, and his meaning is only discoverable by those who have acquired Kierkegaard's light. Nietzsche's road towards existence-philosophy took its rise independently of these two earlier thinkers. Anglo-Saxon pragmatism was for him a sort of preliminary stage. While running atilt against traditional idealism, he seemed to be laying new foundations; but what he built thereon was nothing more than an aggregate of crude analysis of life and cheap optimism, was a mere expression of a blind confidence in the extant confusion.

Existence-philosophy cannot discover any solution, but can only become real in the multiplicity of thought proceeding from extant origins in the communication from one to another. It is timely, but is already more obvious in its failures than in its successes, and has succumbed to the tumultuousness characteristic of the contemporary world.

Existence-philosophy would be instantly lost if it were once more to imply a belief that we know what man is. It would again provide elementary factors for the study of the types of human and animal life, would again become anthropology, psychology, sociology. It can only have a possible significance if it remains unfathomable in its circumstantiality. It awakens what it does not itself know; it illuminates and gives impetus, but it does not fixate. For the man who is on the right road it is the expression thanks to which he is enabled to maintain his direction; it is the instrument whereby he is empowered to safeguard his sublime moments of realisation throughout life.

Existence-philosophy may lapse into pure subjectivity. Then selfhood is misunderstood as the being of the ego, which solipsistically circumscribes itself as life that wishes to be nothing more. But genuine existence-philosophy is that appealing questioning in which, to-day, man is again seeking to come to his true self. Obviously, therefore, it is found only where people wrestle on its behalf. Out of a chance-medley with sociological, psychological, and anthropological thought, it may degenerate into a sophistical masquerade. Now censured as individualism, now used as a justification for personal shamelessness, it becomes the perilous foundation of a hysterical philosophy. But where it remains genuine, where it remains true to itself, it is uniquely effective in promoting all that makes man genuinely human.

The illumination of existence, remaining uncircumstantial, leads to no result. A clarification of consciousness stimulates claims but does not bring fulfilment. As cognitive beings, we have to come to a decision about it. For I am not what I cognise, nor do I cognise what I am. Instead of cognising my existence, I can only inaugurate the process of clarification.

Man's cognition would be at an end if its limits were conceived as those of existence. In the illumination of existence which transgresses the boundaries of cognition a dissatisfaction remains. Upon the basis of the illumination of existence we move into a new dimension when we attempt a metaphysic. The creation of the metaphysically objective world, or the manifestness of the origin of its being, is null if it be divorced from existence. Psychologically regarded, it is only engendered, consists of the forms of fantasy and of peculiarly directed thoughts, of the contents of narration and of the construction of being, which vanish into thin air in face of any attempt at comprehensive knowledge. In it man wins repose, or the clarification of his unrest and his danger, if the genuinely real seems to reveal itself to him.

To-day the prolegomena to metaphysics are, existentially, as confused as is all philosophy. Their possibilities, however, have perhaps become purer even though narrower. Because the cogent knowledge of experience was unexchangeable, metaphysics is no longer possible after the manner of scientific thought, but must be grasped along an entirely different trend. It has, therefore, become more dangerous than before; for it readily leads, either to superstition accompanied by the repudiation of science and sincerity; or else to the perplexity of those who can make no headway because, although they want to know, they find themselves unable to know. Not until these perils upon the foundation of existence-philosophy have been seen and dealt with, does the idea of freedom in the grasping of a metaphysical value become possible. What the millenniums have disclosed to man in the form of transcendentalism could once again become vocal after appropriation or assimilation in a changed form.

PART FIVE

WHAT MANKIND CAN BECOME

1. The Nameless Powers

THE problem of the nameless powers is not the problem of the unknown which can be found and cognised in order to become confronted with a new unknown which again puzzles the searcher. Only beyond the unknown and in contradistinction to it, can man encounter the incomprehensible, which is not the temporarily unknown but the essentially nameless. The nameless which could be grasped would never have been the nameless.

The anonymous, the nameless, is not only the true being of man, which tends to vanish in dispersion, but also the true not-being, which seems, however, to claim the whole realm of life. The problem of the nameless powers is a problem of human existence itself.

To describe namelessness would make an end of it, if description were to become knowledge. But here description is not ascertainment; it is only appealing possibility.

Perversion of Liberty. Modern sophistry displayed manifestations of which the reader must be reminded. The forms of obscurity in mystification, of the revolts of a seeming sincerity, of the uncertainty of opinion and of will, were intended to safeguard the existence of a life-order or to negate it with a convenient straightforwardness. They have created an atmosphere which misleads the life of the individual to flee from itself into a recognised form of activity on behalf of the general good. In the life-order advances are made to me from all sides in order to free me from the claims to selfhood or self-expression.

Positivism, which is relevant only to particular situations, becomes, when rendered absolute in the form of the "new positivism", a mask. In it, people can conceal their own aridity, the individual counting exclusively as a fulfilled function, and losing his validity in the semblance of unlimited jejuneness. They grow afraid of their own words, wishes, and feelings. Nothing remains but technical questions; and when these have been dealt with there ensues a dumbness which is not the profundity of silence but merely an expression of vacancy. Man would like to be able to renounce himself, to plunge into his work as into the waters of oblivion, to be no longer free but merely "natural", as if naturalness were identical with something technically grasped.

Irresoluteness has become the form of that peace which the general interests of the life-order demand. Hence there is a secret struggle between a will that seeks decision concerning true being and the will to a freedom from all trouble and effort, the will to continue an extant life in unchanged forms. This, likewise, would lead into the morass where the possibility of human existence ceases. But the life-order has an easy conscience about the matter, believing that all is right so long as no genuine decisions are asked for.

Yet man cannot surrender himself. As the possibility of freedom, he must either be its true realisation, or else its perversion in which he can find no rest. Entangled in the perversion of freedom, he withers at the roots. We are concerned only with preliminary structures, with transitional forms, with phrase-making.

In this perversion, man turns against liberty. Inspired with a secret love for the being which existed for him as a possibility, he is impelled to destroy it wherever he encounters it. His obscure respect becomes transformed into a profound hatred. He turns the life-order to account that he may, with specious arguments concerning freedom, destroy the reality of this by the might of the apparatus. The essence of freedom is struggle; it does not want to appease but to intensify the contest, does not want to go in leading-strings but to enforce open demonstration. But the nameless enmity to liberty transforms the spiritual struggle into the perverted spirituality of the Inquisition. Ignoring selfhood, taking to flight when it ought to form a strong front, it seizes the first chance of interfering with self-expression or of destroying it by the judgment of one of the official powers. Selfhood is condemned without examination, for, were it left to itself, it would touch us too closely. The study of the innermost springs of behaviour, which belongs to the domain of true communication, becomes in this case the display of private matters for public censure. Only the betrayal of one's own possibility is susceptible of this inquisitorial inquiry, which, in a world devoid of communication, suddenly discloses itself here and there in a surprising way.

In the perversion of liberty, the true consciousness of the relativity of the mere life-order and of the nullity of freedom in face of its transcendency is transformed into a negation of everything. The hidden poison of dissatisfaction with one's own life (a poison for which the life-order provides no antidote) brings to pass a life which is but negational invective instead of action and work. When affected by this virus, all that I wish is to escape everything as it really is that I may not be obliged to face up to it. What should have been a justifiable criticism of times and conditions, because in them man is menaced, becomes a pleasurably sceptical process of annihilation, as if the negative uttered by an incapable were already life. To shatter the world to bits (though of course the fragments will remain, to be shattered once more) is the agreeable purpose of this negation, of this nihilism. Self-consciousness is negatively sought in sacrifice. Nevertheless, owing to the instinctive urge to life, we want, null though we be, to remain ourselves. We deck ourselves out in an inexorable sincerity which at its root is nevertheless falsehood. All the thought which has been part of the epochal consciousness for centuries must serve as tinsel for these negational opinions and utterances.

The Sophist. Every definite view of a perversion is unduly simple, for the perversion of sophistical life is universal. In the very moment when it is being grasped, it has undergone a fresh transformation. The sophist, whose possibility was evolved by the life-order as a nameless warning for the future of man in that order, can only be described as an unceasing perversion. In the very article of formulation he acquires lineaments which are already too definite.

Yet he is never present in an ostensibly natural self-evidence. Well versed in all possibilities, as opportunity arises he seizes now this one and now that one.

He always presents himself as a collaborator, for he wishes to be perpetually on hand. He endeavours to avoid any fundamental conflict, which, if he can get his way, will never become plainly manifest upon any plane. Beneath the veil of an omnipresent inter-connexion, he wants only life, incapable of genuine enmity—which arises on a higher plane of being, in a questioning struggle of destiny against other possi-bilities existing on that same plane.

When everything turns against him, he can cringe and crawl, to resume an erect and defiant posture as soon as the atmosphere grows less threatening. He is able to find an advantageous route even when the prospect is most unfavourable. He enters into rela-tions everywhere, on the assumption that he must necessarily be welcome and that every one will delight in furthering his wishes. He is pliable when vigor-ously resisted; brutal and disloyal when he has the upper hand; pathetic when it costs him nothing; senti-mental when his will is crossed.

If he has won to a strong position, he, who a moment before seemed humble, will now show himself over-weening towards all that has true being. Behind the mask of indignation he manifests his detestation of that which is noble in man. For, whatever happens to him, his persistent aim is the null. Instead of merely admitting the possibility of the null, he has a lively faith in it. This faith impels him, whenever he is confronted by true being, to strive to convince it after his manner that it is null. Consequently, though his knowledge is universal, he is estranged from veneration, shame, and loyalty.

He has an emotional attitude of radical dissatisfac-tion, making, the while, gestures of heroical endurance. Unexistential irony is one of his favourite attitudes.

He is characterless without being malicious, simul-taneously good-humoured and rancorous, at one and the same time obliging and ruthless, and is utterly devoid of sincerity. He commits petty breaches of decorum, is guilty of minor deceptions and frauds, but is also respectable and honourable, though never in the grand style; he is not a consistent devil.

He is never an honest and straightforward adversary, he does not stand firmly on his feet, is persistently forgetful, and knows nothing of an inward sense of responsibility although the word is continually in his mouth. Lacking the independence of unconditioned being, he has the slackness of not-being, in conjunction with the temporary and continually changeful forcibleness of self-assertion.

He finds his true home in intellectualism. There he feels comfortable, for there only can he readily fulfil his task of persistently conceiving the stream of thought as something other than it is. He metamorphoses everything. From lack of selfhood, he can never make science his own; and, according as the situation varies, he vacillates between the superstition of science and the superstition that makes war against science.

He has a passion for discussion. He uses grave and decisive words, adopts radical attitudes, but never stands his ground. He accepts whatever any one else says to him. The other's opinion (he admits) must certainly be quite as sound as his own, but the best thing will be to find a working compromise between the two. Outwardly he sees eye to eye with the other, and then proceeds to act after his own fashion as if nothing whatever had been said.

When he encounters a self-existent adversary, one to whom intellectualism is nothing *per se*, but is valid only as the medium of phenomenal being, he is extraordinarily perturbed, for it seems to him that the validity of his life is threatened. He is therefore continually shifting his outlook, transferring the discussion to a new plane, insisting for a moment upon complete objectivity in order, the next, to give way to his emotions; he makes advances to join hands in a formula as if this must embody the truth; he is lachrymose and angry by turns; never in the same mood or inspired by the same purpose from one moment to another. But, whatever happens, he would rather be annihilated than make no appearance on the stage at all or attract no attention.

It is a vital matter for him that everything should be treated rationally. He accepts modes of thought, categories, and methods without exception, but only as forms of speech, not as embodying the substantial movement of cognition. His thoughts have a syllogistic consistency, so that, by the use of the logical instrument with which every thinker is familiar, he can achieve a momentary success. He makes use of dialectic that he may transform whatever is said into ingenious antitheses; and he riots in intuitions and examples, without ever getting to the root of a matter; luxuriates in crude rationality, since he always talks for effect, and has no concern for true insight. He reckons upon the forgetfulness of those with whom he converses. The emotionalism of his rhetorical professions of resoluteness enables him to slip away like an eel from any resolve which it might trouble him to fulfil. He affirms or rejects just as the fancy takes him. What he says is futility which has no interconnexion with the new succession of time; and communication with him is a plunge into fathomless abysses. Nothing grows out of his words, for they are empty chatter. Those who have anything to do with him are merely wasting their time and their energy. At bottom he is inspired with dread by the awareness of his own nullity, and yet he refuses to take the leap which could bring him to his own true being.

Such descriptions might be continued interminably. They circle round a nameless power which in secret might gain the mastery over all, either in order to transform us into itself, or else in order to exclude us from life.

Problem concerning the Reality of Time. What is contemporarily true being, what being as life is ripe for destruction, what is still in the germ, how both are the fundamentals of the future of human existence— are just as little accessible to knowledge as the being of the sophist. It remains hidden away from us in the realm of silence, and even when he who sustains it plays a public part, it is visible to every one who encounters him, so long as he himself is open to being, which he sees through his own self-existence.

The question as to the reality of time can neither be evaded nor answered. Nothing remains possible to us here but doubts and queries.

We doubt whether this reality has a public existence as that which every one knows and can know, that which from day to day the newspapers print and interpret. For it may exist in that which goes on behind the surface of things; in that which lies beyond the reach of all but the few; and in that to which still fewer have access in their activities. It may perhaps be a life of which no one thinks because no one is really conscious of it.

We doubt whether there can be any spiritual movement in what works so expansively that all can participate in it. Perhaps this accessibility to all is but the overlap of a past movement which, petrified into objectivities, is now subservient to the purposes of entertainment. Unknown to the masses, spiritual movements may at all times have been going on in an invisible realm of the mind. Insofar as human beings secured guidance therefrom, this movement was indirectly effective through supplying the motives of decisions, though not in such a way that its significance became obvious to all, or could become obvious to-day. What was comprehensible to all was the supply of the elementary necessaries of life by means of worldly institutions, the methods of intercommunication by language, the obvious of all kinds—matters with which we are not here concerned.

Doubt arises as to what success really is. Worldly success is made manifest by the amount of public approval, by the obvious effect and validity of what one says, by the acquisition of privileged positions, by the making of money. He who seeks worldly success does so in order to secure an expansion of the conditions of his life; but success first becomes a true success when mastery of the expanded conditions of life becomes a means for true selfhood, for the development of a life fulfilled with all that really makes man man.

What is sketched as a picture of the present is never this present without qualification. Every one lives in a world which presents unknown possibilities. It is, so to say, a law that what one knows has already ceased to be the course of substantial history. The truly real takes place almost unnoticed, and is, to begin with, lonely and dispersed. The new generation at any time is rarely that of which one speaks. Those among our young people who, thirty years hence, will do the things that matter, are, in all probability, now quietly biding their time; and yet, unseen by others, they are already establishing their existence by means of an unrestricted spiritual discipline. They have a feeling for time, and do not anticipate. It is impossible to determine who will be the men of mark in days to come. All attempts at selection are the outcome of the grotesque arrogance of a technical understanding not yet aware of its own limitations. Could we foresee, what we could foresee would already exist, and would need only to be realised by the destiny of a life. There is recognition for talent, diligence, trustworthiness; but not for namelessness as the foreshadowing of true being and as confirmation of worth.

The nameless is wordless, uncertified, unexacting. It is the germ of being in an invisible form, so long as it is still in course of growth and the world cannot yet accord an echo. It is like a flame which may set the world aglow, or may become a mere heap of hot ashes in an incinerated world, though preserving sparks which may start a new flame—or may ultimately return to its source.

Contemporary Man. To-day a hero is not visible. We are shy of the word. Historical decisions are no longer in the hands of isolated individuals, of one who can seize the reins and drive unaided for a time. Decision is absolute only in the personal destiny of the individual, and seems almost always to be no more than relative to the destiny of the contemporary titanic apparatus. Nothing but the mass-man's urgent longing to admire, makes him construct heroes for himself—such heroes as reveal themselves by consummate skill of one sort or another, by venturesomeness, or by acquiring some outstanding political position, so that for a moment an individual occupies the centre of universal attention, but is speedily forgotten when the limelight is turned upon some other figure.

True heroism, so far as it is possible to modern man, is displayed in inconspicuous activity, in the work that does not bring fame. It lacks the confirmation of public approval even though, well adapted to the needs of daily life, it has the power of self-maintenance. It is not bewitched by false expectations, nor are the ears of the hero tickled by the reverberations of applause. He rejects the lure of doing what all can do and what every one will approve, and he is unperturbed by resistance and disapproval. With steady gait, he follows his chosen path. This path is a lonely one, for the dread of calumny and of arrogant disapproval compels most persons to do what will please the crowd. Few are equal to the task of following their own bent without obstinacy and without weakness, of turning a deaf ear to the illusions of the moment, of maintaining without fatigue or discouragement a resolution once formed. In view of the impossibility of self-content, the invisibility of one's own being can only hope for an unverifiable affirmation in the transcendental realm.

If man as hero is characterised by this—that he stands steadfast against the almost overwhelming power which, from generation to generation, works to enforce its blind will against the will of the lonely doer, and which, in each generation, works in a way peculiar to itself—to-day the hero has to safeguard himself against the impalpable masses. The masses must not be radically put to the question by the individual if he wants to continue living in the world. He has silently to endure and to collaborate, unless he is willing to allow himself to be martyred by the despotism of the masses who quietly and inconspicuously destroy. Their power is incorporated in certain individuals each of whom, as a function of a powerful group, temporarily expresses its will (as understood by the leader), carrying out that will for the time being, to become once more a nonentity when the function has been performed. Because they are mere executants of the mass-will, they cannot be grasped as individuals. As a martyr the modern hero would never catch sight of his opponents, and would himself remain invisible as what he really is.

In the scepticism characteristic of our day, the mass-phenomena of superstition have become, so to say, indolent but fanatical ties established through despair. Prophets of all kind have a transient success. The road to independence, however, is by way of an inviolable scepticism towards all that is objectively fixed. The man who, in search of independence, gives expression to true being is radically different from the prophets of an earlier day.

Above all he is not recognised as a prophet, but remains hidden. Were he known as a prophet, he would become a demagogue, an ephemerally idolised and then dismissed leader of the masses, or one who, for a time, would set the fashion for a worshipping group. Knowing this, the true hero will decline the rôle of prophet—will have nothing to do with those who would invest him with the prophet's mantle, for his essence forbids accepting subjugation. He is visible only to the independent, who achieve self-development through contact with his essence. He does not want disciples but companions. Only in State life as the life-destiny of all can he desire followers; here alone will he become a leader as demagogue; and only in the form of a rationality he has himself established will he do that which few really understand and which remains as hidden as he is himself. His essence works indirectly; he does not become a plastic figure; he does not lay down any laws.

Not merged in the enterprise of the coming and going idols of the life-order, he works as self-existence on behalf of self-existence; for he creates life as a demand through influencing others out of their own sources.

He does not predict the future, but describes what is. He grasps this in its abundance as a manifestation of being, without trying to render any sort of myth absolute.

His form is mutable, his objective achievements may be harmless, his recognition may be ambiguous. His essence is an obvious mystery. But the frankness of an unlimited will to see becomes in him a silence; not because he wishes to conceal what he knows and might say, but because he does not wish to drag into the realm of the said what in existence would be obscure to him owing to this inveracity. An inevitable name-lessness is its sign. Every one in his own world must be ready to listen to its appeal, without making it once again invisible by the falsehood of dependence and expectation.

The Struggle with no Fighting Front. The nameless is the true being, and only those who are open to it have assurance against nullity. But, at the same time, the nameless is the life of not-being, whose power is incomparably and incomprehensibly great, although it threatens to destroy everything. The nameless is that in order to become one with which I strive to soar; and it is that against which I have to struggle if I seek being. But this struggle is once more unified. The life of not-being seems to have disappeared, and seems of a sudden to dominate all. It is the straight-forwardly sinister, which promotes unrest through the uncertainty against what and on behalf of what one is fighting. When we are confronted with it there seems nothing left for us but the brutal struggle for life in its extant self-centredness. But this conception is itself inspired by the nameless, which enwraps all in the veil of not-being, because it is itself a nullity.

Just as primitive man believed himself to stand face to face with demons and believed that could he but know their names he would become their master, so is contemporary man faced by this incomprehensible, which disorders his calculations. "If I can but grasp it, if I can but cognise it," so he thinks, "I can make it my servant." The nameless powers of the null are, in our world whence the gods have been driven forth, the analogy of the demons that confronted primitive man.

A fight in which we know with whom we have to do is a plain matter enough. But in the modern life-order, after a phase of temporary clearness, we are afflicted by the confusion of the fighting front. He who just now seemed our opponent, has become our ally. What in accordance with the objectivity of our voluntary expectations ought to be our adversary, joins forces with us; what seems really antagonistic, lays down its arms; what looked like a united front is divided against itself. All this occurs in a medley and amid a turbulent interchange. It makes my nearest neighbour my enemy and some one at the other side of the world my companion at arms.

We might fancy that this state of affairs must be the outcome of the struggle between two generations which is now being fought out; in this sense, that the individual does not know where he stands, and no one can know what is obsolete and what is the substance of the future. The essence of the epoch is obscure, and it seems possible that, misunderstanding ourselves and the situation, we may fight against our own true purposes. Yet there exists no unity, neither that of a past nor that of a future epoch. The essence of man in his history is, rather, a perpetual betwixt and between, rather than the unrest of a life which is at any particular time incomplete. A search for the unity of the coming generation cannot help him; but perhaps he can aid himself by the persistent endeavour to unveil from moment to moment the nameless powers which are simultaneously inimical to the life-order and to selfhood.

Man would gladly pass from casual and undesired fighting fronts to the genuine ones on which he is eager to struggle. He would like the fronts which disclose themselves as mere outworks because they are not animated by any all-pervading will, to collapse; he would fain catch sight of his genuine adversaries. That which incomprehensibly intervenes, troubles the clarity of vision, paralyses the will, obscures the goal. Why does not it reveal itself? Only when I myself and the other understand one another in the fight does this become full of meaning. I want clear consciousness, so that I can discern my opponent. He ought not to hide behind my back and vanish into the distance when I turn to face him; he ought to look me in the eyes and answer my challenge. But the nameless powers slip away and metamorphose themselves. If for a moment I seem to grasp them, it is only to find that they are no longer what they were. In many configurations they cease to be a power if one does not offer any resistance to them but simply leaves them alone; but then, unexpectedly, they turn up in a new form. They are just as ready to pose as enemies and as friends, being equally ambiguous in the one rôle and in the other. No one who has set out seriously in search of the unconditioned can have failed to encounter these spooks. They do their utmost to render our purposive life futile, and they undermine man's selfhood. In other instances, man fights among the shadows and helps them in their campaign without being aware of the fact.

Genuine adversaries are found where being contends with being for a productive struggle in life. But there are no adversaries where being wrestles with not-being for life. Behind our backs it may happen that not-being masquerading as life triumphs in the incomprehensible configurations of sophistry.

2. MAINTENANCE OF SELFHOOD IN THE CONTEMPORARY SITUATION

The modality of human existence is the presupposition of everything. Apparatus may be perfected as much as you please, but if men of the right sort are lacking, it is of no avail. If man is not to be allowed to founder in the mere persistence of life, it may seem essential that in his consciousness he shall be confronted with the null; he must recall his origin. Whereas at the outset of his historical course he was in danger of being physically annihilated by the natural forces, now his very being is menaced by a world he has himself established. Though upon another level than in the unknown beginnings of his development, his whole being is again at stake.

Neither an exuberant joy of life nor yet a resolute endurance of nullity can save him. Both are doubtless indispensable as temporary refuges in time of trouble; but they do not suffice.

If man is to be himself, he needs a positively fulfilled world. When his world has fallen into decay, when his ideas seem to be dying, man is so long hidden from himself that he becomes unable on his own initiative to discover the ideals that confront him in the world.

But with the self-existence of the individual there begins that which then for the first time realises itself to become a world. Even though this should seem to have become hopeless in an unspiritual life-order, there remains in man as a pure possibility that which has momentarily receded out of sight. If to-day we ask in our despair what is still left for us in this world, to every one there comes the answer: "That which you are, because you can." The mental situation to-day compels man, compels every individual, to fight wittingly on behalf of his true essence. He must either maintain it or lose it according to the way in which he becomes aware of the foundation of his being in the reality of his life.

The present moment seems to be one which makes extensive claims, makes claims it is almost impossible to satisfy. Deprived of his world by the crisis, man has to reconstruct it from its beginnings with the materials and presuppositions at his disposal. There opens to him the supreme possibility of freedom, which he has to grasp even in face of impossibility, with the alternative of sinking into nullity. If he does not pursue the path of self-existence, there is nothing left for him but the self-willed enjoyment of life amid the coercions of the apparatus against which he no longer strives. He must either on his own initiative independently gain possession of the mechanism of his life, or else, himself degraded to become a machine, surrender to the apparatus. He must, through communication, establish the tie between self and self, in full awareness that here everything turns upon loyalty or disloyalty; and in default of this his life will be utterly despiritualised and become a mere function. He must either advance to the frontier where he can glimpse his transcendentalism, or else must remain entangled in the disillusionment of a self that is wholly involved in the things of the world. The demands made of him are such as assume him to have the powers of a titan. He must meet these demands, and must see what he is capable of in the way of self-development; for, if he fails to do so, there will remain for him nothing but a life in which he will have the advantages neither of man nor of beast.

It boots nothing to complain that too much is being laid upon the individual, and that circumstances ought to be altered. Effective work upon environing conditions can only arise out of the modality of selfhood. I am unfaithful to my own possibilities when I await from a change of circumstances what I can do on my own initiative. I shirk my task when I impose upon another what is incumbent on myself; and this other can only thrive when I myself become all that I am capable of being.

Against the World or in the World. The first sign of awakening circumspection in the individual is that he will show a new way of holding himself towards the world. Selfhood or self-existence first arises out of his being against the world in the world.

The first step leads out of the world into solitude. Self-existence which, in the negative resolve for self-renunciation, fails to grasp any world-existence, consumes itself in possibility. It can only speak in order to question things. To create unrest is its element. This method of Kierkegaard's, which was inevitable as a phase in the transition, would become insincere if a man firmly established on his own foundations were to promote unrest for others. Any one who, while carrying on an occupation, takes a positive grasp of life, who acts as a teacher, has a family, lives in a world of historical and scientific knowledge because he finds this more relevant, has abandoned the path of the unworldliness of negative resolve. He cannot wish to snatch the ground from under the feet of others without showing them the ground on which he himself stands.

The second path leads into the world, but only by way of the possibility of the first path. For philosophising self-existence cannot stand fast in its world with unquestioning satisfaction.

To-day, when the complications of all life in the apparatus can no longer be swept away, when life has become an enterprise in which the great majority of persons are workers and employees, it is futile to expect a profession or means of livelihood in which one will be independent of others. Participation in the community of interests and of labour of all those who pursue the same occupation or practise the same means of earning a livelihood, a participation that will safeguard one's own life subject to externally imposed purposes and conditions, is now unavoidable. There are, of course, still vestiges of comparatively independent enclaves, relics of the past, which it may be well to preserve, whenever they are found, as precious possibilities handed down from antiquity and capable of disclosing an irreplaceable type of human existence; but for almost all it is now inevitable to work in a joint enterprise or to perish. The question is how to live in such an enterprise.

Ambiguously alluring is the possibility of setting oneself exclusively against the world. He only can sincerely renounce it who condemns himself to suffer shipwreck in face of all realisation. For if, while trying to turn to the best account a favourable economic situation life offers him, he nevertheless keeps himself to himself utterly apart from the world, he sinks into a vacancy in which he still remains a prey to the world; he becomes insincere in his flight from the world which, while railing against it, he only eludes in order, through negating it, to count still as being.

The reality of the world cannot be evaded. Experience of the harshness of the real is the only way by which a man can come to his own self. To play an active part in the world, even though one aims at an impossible, an unattainable goal, is the necessary precondition of one's own being. What we have to endeavour, therefore, is to live at harmony with the powers of this world without being absorbed by them. The enterprise in its restriction to the region of the indispensable retains its preponderance, a solidarised attempt to further the provision of the elementary necessaries of human life for all remaining the field of activity for the individual likewise—the individual participating in this work because all are engaged in it in order to make life possible. But the ethos of this labour excludes the dread of self-existence.

The degradation of the field of labour to become merely relative would seem to annul one's pleasure in using one's energies; and yet it is the existence of man to be able to persist in this jejune activity without any paralysis of the will-to-do. For selfhood is only possible in virtue of this tension, thanks to which, instead of merely juxtaposing two vital domains, we try to bring it about that one shall be fulfilled with the other, even though a universally valid form of unification as the only desirable life for all be impossible. Thus we have to live, as it were, upon a narrow mountain ridge, falling away on one side into the mere enterprise, or, on the other, into a life devoid of reality side by side with the enterprise.

The significance of entering into the world constitutes the value of philosophy. True, philosophy is not an instrument, and still less is it a talisman; but it is awareness in the process of realisation. Philosophy is the thought with which or as which I am active as my own self. It is not to be regarded as the objective validity of any sort of knowledge, but as the consciousness of being in the world.

Technical Sovereignty, Primary Will, Unconditioned Ties. The entry of the selfhood into its world is to be contemplated in its possible trend. From the technical, the road leads by way of the primary will to the unconditioned ties.

(*a*) Everyday complications of a technicised world make it necessary for me to master these complications in the environment accessible to me. The relationship to things has been transformed; as a further remove there remain, in their indifference, nothing more than transferable functions; technique has divorced man from the immediate present. The new task is, with the methods of technical realisation, to come once again into the direct presence of human existence as regards all things in the world. The new presupposition of intensified possibilities must be pressed into our service. The rationalisation of the means of life, including a rationalised distribution of our time and a rationalised economising of our energies, must restore to every individual (in virtue likewise of his own spontaneous effort) the possibility of being thoroughly contemporary; so that he can reflect about, so that he can allow to ripen, so that he can enter into genuine contact with, the things which are his own. The new possibility is not merely an objectively secure engrossment with the purposive mechanical realisation of the material conditions of life, but the attainment thereby of a freedom that shall enable us to rise superior to all material considerations.

Wherever the realm of technique has been conquered, man's enthusiasm concerning discoveries that make him the originator of a transformation of the world, that make him, so to say, a second great architect of the world, is the privilege of those who have advanced to the limits of the attainable.

Where technique is being utilised, the appropriate attitude is a restriction to the necessary minimum of effort, the economising of time, deliberate movements which waste no energy. Notwithstanding the apparently bewildering complication of the technical world, there becomes possible a peculiar tranquillity which dominates the objective conditions of life and the vital activities of the doer. Obedience to the laws of orderly functioning, in which people are trained from childhood upward, provides free space for selfhood as well.

The world of technique seems destructive to the natural world. People complain that life has become unnatural. Artificial technique, which in the course of its development has had to put up with much ugliness and has had to accept a severance from nature, might in the end provide a more effective access to nature in general. Modern man is able to enjoy the sunshine and the play of the elements with a new awareness of them. Technique supplies the possibility of a life which can be passed in any part, in many parts, of the geographical world; of a life wherein it has become increasingly possible to enjoy light and air and all their manifestations. Since everything has become close and accessible, the limits of the home have been greatly expanded. Thanks to this conquest of nature there has increased a true delight in nature undefiled, which the activities of my body enable me to attain to, enjoy, and ardently perceive as lord of the senses five. Insofar as I avail myself and expand this revelation in the environment directly vouchsafed to me, and insofar as I keep my feet firmly planted upon the ground (using the revelation as no more than one of the technical instruments to bring me into closer contact with the universal mother), I am enabled—in these artificially created possibilities—not merely to see the cipher of nature more distinctly, but also to read it better.

Technicisation is a path along which we have no choice but to advance. Any attempt to retrace our steps would mean that life would be rendered increasingly difficult until it would become impossible. Invective is of no use here; we have to overcome. The world of technique, therefore, must be taken as a matter of course; so much so that all which goes on within it must lie almost outside the field of active attention. As contrasted with the need that all our activities must be more successfully grounded upon advanced technique, we have to cultivate our awareness of the non-mechanisable to the pitch of infallibility. To render the world of technique absolute would be destructive of selfhood, and therefore our sense of the value of technical achievement must be permeated with a new significance.

(b) The system whereby the elementary necessaries of human life are provided, demands knowledge only for utilitarian purposes. Selfhood in knowledge, on the other hand, is a primary will to know. Here we are concerned with a longing for knowledge for its own sake. If I accept utility as the ultimate standard of knowledge, I surrender my own selfhood therein.

But if knowledge be pursued for its own sake, in the pursuit I achieve self-awareness.

Utilitarian knowledge is only possible as an outcome of that genuine knowledge which undergoes segregation and contemplates itself as something set apart in the world of the cogently valid and actual. Consequently, even in the technical life-order, a decisive sense for the modality of the known is only trustworthy where there is a selfhood which sets limits. In default of this, there arises a confusion of the known and the imaginary. If rationally cogent knowledge be rendered absolute, all being is contemplated as lying within the realm of technique, with the result of a misunderstanding that gives rise to the superstition of science, and ere long to every sort of superstition. For under such conditions man can neither cognise in a trustworthy fashion nor yet be truly himself, seeing that science can only comprehend that which it itself primarily is.

The future lies where the tension of the modalities of knowledge is maintained. In such conditions, special knowledge would still be illuminated by being, and philosophy would be fulfilled by the singularity of the world. Selfhood is the supreme instrument of knowledge, an instrument which indeed supplies vision only according to the degree in which it takes cognisance of the world, but also only insofar as it itself remains active. Life becomes for the individual the responsibility of the human being aware of himself as being, and, in addition and simultaneously, the experiment of the knower. What man does investigatively, purposively, and constructively, is (regarded in its entirety) the road of endeavour on which he discovers his destiny and the manner in which he becomes aware of being.

(c) But life as mere life, the life that proceeds in a succession of passing moments until it comes to its term, has no destiny; for it, time is no more than a series, remembrance is indifferent; the present (having no continuity with the future) is nothing more than a momentary enjoyment or a momentary failure to achieve enjoyment. Man wins destiny only through ties: not through coercive ties imposed on him as an impotent creature by great forces that lie without; but by ties freely comprehended which he makes his own. Such ties hold his life together, so that it is not frittered away but becomes the actuality of his possible existence. Then remembrance discloses to him its indelible foundations; and the future reveals to him the region wherein he will be held accountable for what he does to-day. Life grows indefinitely vast. From moment to moment, he has his epoch, his realisation, his maturity, his possibility. Selfhood exists as a life which wishes to become an aggregate, and as such secures valid ties only through the doer.

The melting away of historical interconnexions until they become a mere heap of individuals replaceable at will as functions in the apparatus, tends to disintegrate man into the brief perspective of the contemporary present. Interconnexion is then purely relative; it is forfeitable, no more than temporary, and the unconditioned is regarded as a merely unconcrete emotionalism. Amid this positivism, the sense of chaos grows. That is why, to-day, people are continually demanding new ties, are in search of authority and of ecclesiastical faith. But even though time can work wonders, genuine ties cannot be artificially established; they must be freely engendered by the individual in community life. If the demand for ties is nothing more than a demand for an artificial order in obedience to authority and written law, the real task is being evaded, the upshot being that the unconditioned becomes impossible and freedom is paralysed. Man, therefore, is faced by two alternatives. Either he must seek appeasement in forgetfulness of life and in a return to authoritative forms which can sanctify the apparatus for supplying the elementary needs of human life; or else, as an individual, he must grasp the very foundations by building upon which an exclusive unconditioned always determines life.

He alone can remain sincere in the world who lives by means of something genuinely acquired which he can only get by way of ties. Revolt against objective ties, therefore, as purely negational, is insincere, culminates in an eternal chaos, and is apt to persist when the purpose of the revolt no longer obtains: it is only sincere, it is only true, as the struggle of freedom for breathing-space; is justified only by the energy of an endeavour to form ties.

Historical Immersion. He only who freely enters into ties is thereby endowed with the power of revolting despairingly against himself. The unfulfillable and yet only task left for contemporary man as man, has been, in face of the null, to find the true path at his own risk, the path on which life will once more become a whole, notwithstanding all its dispersal in the restlessness of prevailing commotions. As in the days of the mythical heroes of antiquity, everything seems thrust back upon the individual.

But what is requisite is that a man, in conjunction with other men, should merge himself in the world as a historically concrete entity, so that, amid the universal homelessness, he may win for himself a new home. His remoteness from the world sets him free to immerse his being. This remoteness is not achievable by an intellectualist abstraction, but only through a simultaneous getting into touch with all reality. The immersion is not a visible act of one who plumes himself on it, but is effected in a tranquil unconditionedness. Remoteness from the world gives an inward distinction; but immersion, on the other hand, awakens all that is human in selfhood. The former demands self-discipline; but the latter is love.

True, this historical immersion, which the unconditionedness of possible existence can achieve in virtue of ties, is not to be effected in accordance with any prescription; we can only speak of it as an appeal. It is to be encountered in the energy of veneration, as concentration in occupational work, and as exclusivity in erotic love.

The energy of veneration holds firmly to the standard of what man is and can be, sustaining itself by the contemplation of great historical figures. It does not admit that what is thus disclosed to it can perish from out the world. It is loyal to whatever has been effective in its self-becoming as tradition. It comprehends that out of which its being has grown in the particular person in whose shadow it first became aware of itself; and it persists as a pious affection which never wanes. Remembrance preserves for it as an absolute claim that which no longer has any real existence in the world. Even though what the individual now encounters in life seems almost always to lack value and distinction, and even though disillusionment be heaped upon disillusionment, still he has to preserve as far as may be the standard of his own essence, to find indications for his path amid the dispersed embers of the true, and to become certain where it is that man is really man.

Work and nothing but work performed day after day will, when performed, sink forthwith into the fathomless abysses of oblivion. But it will become a manifestation of selfhood when it is actively performed under the impulsion of long views, when he who does the work works constructively, with his mind concentrated upon the continuity of his will to work and upon his awareness of its trend. Even if he be unable to escape the curse of unemployment, or if his labour power be perforce applied to ends against which his inner being revolts, still there remains to him the standard of his own essence, the question how far, even in this last poverty, he can by his own activity still achieve a nearness to things; and there endures a possibility hard to fulfil, a truth never to be demanded from others, namely the recognition, "Although I am an anvil, as a hammer I can consummate what I must suffer."

Exclusiveness in the love of the sexes binds two human beings together unconditionally for the whole of their future. It is unfathomably rooted in the decision which links the self to this fidelity at the moment when it really became aware of itself through the other. The negative renunciation of polygamous eroticism is the outcome of a positive which, as contemporary love, is only sincere when it includes the whole of life; and the negative determination not to squander oneself is the outcome of an uncompromising readiness for this loyalty on the part of a possible selfhood. Without strictness in erotic matters, there is no selfhood; but eroticism becomes first truly human through the exclusiveness of unconditional ties. When desire breathes a flattering tale, when some inward monitor seems to tell us that the charm of erotic fulfilment and individual happiness are only to

be found in a succession of diversified sexual experiences, the standard of true humanhood remains in the
power we have to refrain from stooping to this lure,
and to refuse our recognition to the demands of
uncontrolled nature.

Veneration is, as it were, the foundation of selfhood; occupational activity is its possible realisation
in the world; and exclusive love of an individual or
an unconditional readiness for such love is the sincerity
of the spirit of selfhood, without which we lapse into
invincible brutalism.

Every search for the unconditioned makes man, so
to say, unnatural in his severity towards himself; for
the genuineness of a being that is historically irreplaceable is associated with an immense exercise of self-
restraint, with a vigorous control of the will. He
only who uses an unbending force of self-discipline,
sustained by an urgent feeling for the possibility of
true fulfilment, walks along the road proper to man
as man—a road primarily entered upon under the
coercion of objective authority, but now deliberately
and freely chosen by the self become aware of its own
responsibility.

This liberty in historical immersion, unconditioned,
is, as far as the real life of the masses is concerned,
associated with the existence of the authority of
spiritual powers. The tension between freedom and
authority is of such a kind that each would become
annulled were it not for the existence of the other;
liberty becoming chaos, and authority becoming
despotism. Selfhood, therefore, cherishes the conservative forces against which, at one time, it had to
come into its own as an individual. It wants the
tradition which, for all spiritual life, is solidly embodied
only in authoritative figures. Although there is no

freedom in the Church, the Church, nonetheless, is a necessary condition of such liberty as is at any time attainable. It preserves the extent of spiritual value, a feeling for the inexorability of transcendental reality, the urgency of the claims which the transcendental makes upon man. Great would be the dangers attendant upon its unnoted decay to become part of the mass-apparatus in tacit alliance with unfaith and with the consequent loss of that which it still possesses competent to function once again as a source of freedom.

Man's Nobility. The question whether human worth be still possible is identical with the question whether human nobility be still possible. There is no longer any question of aristocracy in the form of the rule of a minority of persons who hold their privileged position merely in virtue of inheritance, of a stratum which is uplifted above the crowd by power, possessions, education, and a realised cultural ideal; of those who regard their dominion as the best thing for the community, and whose dominion is accepted as best by the masses. Seldom indeed could any such dominion remain for long a true aristocracy, a genuine rule by the best. Even though for a brief space an aristocracy which held its position upon sociological or biological grounds has done great work, it soon decays into the enforced rule of a minority of persons who, themselves constituting a mass, come to display the typical lineaments of the mass, namely decision by majorities, hatred of any outstanding individuals, a demand for equality, the relentless isolation or exclusion of any notable peculiarities which are not characteristic of the crowd, the persecution of the pre-eminent. Aristocracy as the dominion of a minority-mass arrogates to itself, to all who belong to this ruling minority, qualities which are but sociological substitutes for the true nobility of human existence. If again and again such an aristocracy has created a unique spiritual world, this has been owing to its origin from a true nobility and to a long-lasting process of self-education.

Sociologically there will perhaps continue to exist powerful strata, but they will be ·barbaric. The problem of human nobility to-day is how we are to rescue the reality of the best, who constitute a very small minority.

Such an aristocracy cannot hold itself aloof from the world, cannot realise its true self through the cultivation of personal life inspired by a romantic love for the past. It would be nothing more than the artificial segregation of a group putting forward unwarrantable claims, unless it were deliberately and with a full exercise of the conscious will to participate in the vital conditions of the epoch, wherein, in fact, its being is rooted.

The best in the sense of the nobility of human existence are not merely the talented who might be cultivated by selection, are not racial types whose existence might be determined by anthropological canons, are not persons of genius who have created works altogether out of the common—but, among all of these, are persons who are themselves, in contradistinction to those who feel in themselves a mere vacancy, who recognise no cause for which to fight, who are in flight from themselves.

To-day there is beginning the last campaign against the nobility. Instead of being carried on upon a political and sociological plane, it is conducted in the realm of mind. People would gladly turn the course of developments backward; would check that unfolding of personality which was regarded as fundamental to times which, though recent, are already forgotten. The urgency of the problem how we are best to care for the mass-man who is not willing to stand firmly on his own feet, has led to a revolt of the existential plebeianism in each one of us against the selfhood which the Godhead (though concealed) demands from us. The possibility that the individual shall come to his own self in the course of his destiny is to be definitively destroyed. The instincts of the masses make common cause—as they have often done before, but now more dangerously than ever—with religio-ecclesiastical and politico-absolutist instincts, to furnish a consecration for the universal levelling-down in the mass-order.

This revolt is directed against what is truly noble in man. Earlier revolts, political revolts, could succeed without ruining man; but this revolt, were it to be successful, would destroy man. For not merely during recent centuries but throughout historical times since the days of the Jewish prophets and the Greek philosophers, human existence has been shown to depend upon that which nowadays we term individuality or personality. Whatever we call it, it is objectively incomprehensible, is the always unique and irreplaceable modality of selfhood.

Solidarity. When men are huddled together like dust in a heap, reality and certainty exist where friends are true friends in the factual communication of their manifestations and in the solidarity of personal loyalty.

What frees us from solitude is not the world, but the selfhood which enters into ties with others. Interlinkage of self-existent persons constitutes the invisible reality of the essential. Since there is no objective criterion of trustworthy selfhood, this could not be directly assembled to form influential groups.   As has been well said: "There is no trust (no organised association) of the persons who are the salt of the earth." That is their weakness, inasmuch as their strength can only inhere in their inconspicuousness.   There is among them a tie which does not take the form of any formal contract, but is stronger than any national, political, partisan, or social community, and stronger than the bonds of race.   Never direct and immediate, it first becomes manifest in its consequences.

The best gift the temporary world can give us is this approximation of self-existent human beings. They are, in fact, themselves the guarantee that being exists.   In the world are to be found the figures of those who have influenced me as reality; not the transient creatures who were mere acquaintances, but the enduring personalities who made me aware of myself.   There no longer exists a pantheon, but there is a place set apart in the imagination for the remembrance of genuine human beings, of those whom we have to thank for being what we are.   The persons who are decisive for us are, primarily, not those who are merely known as the "great men" of history; but these great ones in proportion as they have been, so to say, reincarnated in the living who have exerted an effective influence upon us.   The latter are for us (who have confident assurance of their proximity) enduring though unexacting—without idolisation and without propaganda.   They are not conspicuous among those who are recognised by the masses of the public and by them regarded as the persons who count, and yet it is upon them that the proper course of affairs depends.

True nobility is not found in an isolated being.

It exists in the interlinkage of independent human beings. Such are aware of their duty to discover one another, to help one another onward wherever they encounter one another, and to be ever ready for communication, on the watch, but without importunacy. Though they have entered into no formal agreement, they hold together with a loyalty which is stronger than any formal agreement could give. This solidarity extends even to an enemy when selfhood comes into genuine opposition with selfhood. Thus there is realised that which, for instance, might exist in political parties across all divergencies as a solidarity of the best—palpable even when it does not come to open expression because there is no occasion for it or because its development is obstructed by the chances of the situation.

The solidarity of these persons has to be distinguished from the universally arising preferences dependent upon sympathy and antipathy; from the peculiar attractive force which all mediocrities exercise on one another because it is congenial to them to be among those who do not make lofty demands; and from the feeble but persistent and passive holding together of the many against the few. Whereas all of these latter categories feel themselves more secure because they exist as and encounter one another as masses and deduce their rights from mass-power, the solidarity of the self-existent is infinitely more assured in its personal trustworthiness even so far as the unobjectified and unobjectifiable minutiæ of behaviour are concerned, but is rendered insecure in the world by the weakness due to the comparatively small number of such persons and to the uncertainty of their contacts. The others, those of the mass-categories, have dozens of men as friends who are not really friends; but a member of the élite is lucky if he has but one friend.

The nobility of the self-existent spirit is widely scattered, the individuals that combine to form it being separated by great intervals. One who enters that nobility does not elect himself to it by an act of judgment, but enters it through the realisation of his own being. The unity of this dispersed élite is like the Invisible Church of a *corpus mysticum* in the anonymous chain of the friends from among whom, here and there, and through the objectivity of individual activities, one selfhood is revealed to another and perhaps distant selfhood. In this immaterial realm of mind there are, at any moment, a few indwellers who, entering into close proximity, strike flame out of one another by the intimacy of their communication. They are the origin of the loftiest soaring movement which is as yet possible in the world. They alone constitute true human beings.

Nobility and Politics. The masses first enter into movement thanks to leaders who tell them what they (the masses) want. Minorities make history. But it is improbable to-day that the masses would retain their veneration for an aristocracy even though they should recognise that the members of this aristocracy form a body of persons who have a right to rule. No doubt it is needful that to-day all those who, owing to the lack of true selfhood, are unable to think sincerely, should nevertheless acquire and busy themselves with the grammar of thought. But the masses, having in this way learned a little, having in this way come to participate a little in thought, are continually eager to participate in political action.

The question therefore arises how a minority put into power by the momentary assent of the masses is to fashion for itself the instruments of authority whereby then, even when assent is withdrawn, it can maintain its dominion in order to impress upon the mass-man the desired stamp, though the mass-man has no true self and does not know what he really wants. Exclusive minorities, aware of their own nobility, may join forces in order to seize power in a State, doing so under the name of the vanguard, of the most advanced, of those endowed with the most energetic wills, or as the retainers of a great leader, or on the ground of privileges of blood. They range themselves like the sects of old days, exerting a vigorous selection upon their own ranks, imposing high demands, exercising strict control. They feel themselves to be an élite, striving to preserve themselves as such after acquiring power, and for this purpose training up a younger generation of successors who are to perpetuate their authority. Nevertheless, even though in their origination the energy of selfhood as the nobility of man may have played a part and may continue to play a part in the most decisive individuals, the generality of such a ruling caste soon becomes a new and by no means aristocratic mass as a minority. There seems to be really no hope—in an epoch when the influence of the mass-man is decisive—that the nobility of human existence shall persist in the form of a ruling minority.

It follows, therefore, that the problem of nobility versus the masses is no longer a specifically political problem. The two, of course, still appear as antitheses in political argumentation, but it is only the words that are the same as of old, for the things signified are heterogeneous—whether an organised minority rules in defiance of the larger masses, or the nobility works anonymously in the mass-order; whether an unjustified and therefore intolerable form of rule becomes definitively established, or whether the nobility of human existence finds scope for realisation.

False Claim to Nobility. Since nobility is manifested only in the soaring movement wherein being strives to realise itself, nobility cannot furnish its own predicate. It is not a species to which one belongs and another does not belong, but man at large in the possibility of his uplift. Because ·we are prone to find our satisfaction in mere life, the energy of the soaring movement is always confined to a few, but even in them not definitively so confined. They are not the representatives of the masses as the climax of mass-being, but, rather, their obscure reproach. Only as misunderstood do they become known to the masses.

The notion of equality, as apart from a mere metaphysical primary possibility, and as considered in relation to the actual life of man, is inveracious, and is therefore almost always silently rejected. The physiognomically repulsive in demeanour and aspect, hateful laughter, detestable self-satisfaction, unworthy plaintiveness, the emotional conviction that one is strong only in association with the masses—he alone who feels in tune with the base can fail to be repelled by such things. No man can contemplate his image in the mirror without some perplexity or dismay; and the more vigorously he aspires, the more sensitive will he be to the presence of other than aspiring elements in himself. The masses are to be recognised insofar as they serve, achieve, look upward towards the impulse of a possible ascent; this meaning, insofar as they themselves are that which the few are to a much more decisive degree. It is not man as an instance of life, but man as possible existence, who is worthy to be loved—as the nobility potentially present in every individual.

But if the nobility in man wishes to understand itself as a definite life and wishes to choose itself, it fortifies itself. Genuine nobility is anonymous in the form of man's claim on himself, whereas spurious nobility is a pose and the making of claims on others.

In answer, therefore, to the question whether an aristocracy is possible to-day, we can only appeal to the man who moots this question, to his own self. This is the spiritual campaign which goes on in every individual, unless he be palsied once for all.

The Philosophical Life. The nobility of human existence may be termed the philosophical life. He is ennobled who is tinged by the sincerity of a faith. One, indeed, who leaves to an authority that which he can only be himself, forfeits his nobility; but one who has trust in the Godhead does not lose himself, for he experiences the truth of his soaring movement as a movement of the finite self-existence even in failure—a truth thanks to which all that happens to him in the world cannot be anything more than he is himself.

It is primarily a matter of tradition that nobility of this sort is still demanded. We cannot achieve everything in outward activity; and as far as inward activity at the centre of human things is concerned what is needed is a word which is not an empty word but can be the awakening of that which is yet to come. The word undergoes transformation, but is the secret clue by which true human existence feels its way into the coming time. As the philosophical life, this human existence (without which the soul is lacking to the objective reality of life in the world) is the ultimate significance of philosophical thought.

In it alone is systematic philosophy tested and confirmed.

Man's future resides in the modality of his philosophical life. This is not to be regarded as a prescription in accordance with which he has to guide himself, nor yet as an ideal type towards which he has to converge. The philosophical life is not, speaking generally, a unique thing, identical for all. It is like a star-shower, a myriad meteors, which, knowing not whence they come nor whither they go, shoot through life. The individual will join in the movement, to however small an extent, through the soaring of his self-existence.

The Situation of the Selfhood. Man does not arrive at an end of his development; it is an essential part of his being that, as time goes on, he should perpetually change in the progress towards an ever new destiny. From the outset, each of his configurations in the world which, for the time, he has brought into being, bears within it the germs of its own ruin.

After history has driven him out of one form of life into the next, out of one awareness of his being into another, he can remember having passed from the previous phase to the present one, but it seems to him as if he could advance no farther along the road. Never since the beginning of his days does man seem to have realised that he is faced by the null, and that it is incumbent upon him through his remembrance of the past to carve out a new path for himself.

To-day, although the possibilities of an expansion of life have become immeasurable, we feel ourselves to be in so narrow a strait that our existential possibility is deprived of its breadth. Since this has been generally realised, a sense of despair has affected human activity (or, as regards those who do not realise it, an unconsciousness)—a sense of despair which, objectively regarded, might just as well herald an end as a beginning.

Man cannot evade this situation, cannot return to forms of consciousness which are unreal because they belong to the days of the past. He might tranquillise himself in the self-forgetful pleasures of life, fancying himself to have gone back to nature in the peace of timelessness. But one day iron reality would again confront him and paralyse him.

For the individual, thrust back into his own nudity, the only option to-day is to make a fresh start in conjunction with the other individuals with whom he can enter into a loyal alliance. The stirring reports of the way in which, during the last phases of the Great War when our western front was crumbling, here and there some of our men stood firm, and, as self-sacrificing individuals, effected what no command could have made them do, actually and at the last moment safeguarding the soil of the fatherland against destruction and storing up for German memories a consciousness of invincibility—these reports disclose an otherwise scarcely attained reality as a symbol of contemporary possibilities. Here was the first human existence which, in face of the null, in face of destruction, was able to realise, no longer its own world, but a world which would belong to future generations.

If we term the condition of those confronted with the null "unfaith", then the energy of the selfhood in unfaith engenders an inward activity which promotes a soaring movement in face of that which is hidden from sight. This energy scorns to shift on to objective causes that which must spring from internal freedom or fail of its effect. It regards itself

230

as called to the highest, and lives in the tension of a cogency, in a forcible revolt against mere life, in the pliability of the relative, in the patience of one who has the capacity for waiting, in the exclusiveness of a historical tie. It knows that it is failing, and, in the act of failure, reads the cipher of being. It is the faith which is grounded in philosophy, the faith which, enabling each individual that succumbs to hand on the torch to another, unceasingly regenerates itself.

No term can be set to this movement. Perpetually it enables us to see what man is or can be. In every moment wherein a human being moves forward on his path under the spur of the unconditioned, there is in time that which annihilates time.

The past cannot tell him how he is to conduct himself. Though illuminated by the light of a remembered past, he has to decide for himself. At length it becomes clear to him what his mental situation is; in what vesture he becomes aware and assured of being; what he unconditionally wants; to whom, in the extant situation, he is to turn, and whose voice, speaking to him in the inner man, he shall listen to.

Unless he draws from these sources, the world remains for him mere enterprise. If his being is to become a true world, the man who, in community life, is to give himself up to a whole must first of all grasp himself.

Self-existence or selfhood is the condition in default of which the world as the reality of human activity, a reality permeated by an ideal, is no longer possible. Because selfhood exists only in unity with the being of the time, it is still resolutely determined to live only in this same time even though it should find itself· in conflict therewith. Every act of its realisation becomes the germ, however small, of the creation of a new world.

3. CONTEMPLATIVE FORECAST AND ACTIVE FORECAST

Contemplative Forecast. As compared with the thousands of millions of years since the beginning of the world, the six thousand years of human tradition seem no more than the first second of a new period in the transformation of our planet. As contrasted with the hundreds of thousands of years during which (as disinterred skulls and other bones show) man has lived upon the earth, written and traditional history are but the earliest beginnings of what man can become as soon as he sets himself in movement to escape from slothfully recurrent conditions. No doubt from the outlook of a species for which thirty years are a generation, six thousand years is a long time. Man's memory makes him aware of the age of his race, so that now, just as two thousand years ago, he feels himself to be living in a terminal period, and he is apt to fancy that his best days lie in the past. But perspectives of terrestrial history have made him aware of the brevity of his undertakings and of the situation which has prevailed since he became man. He knows, now, that all lies in front of him. The speed of technical advances from decade to decade seems an infallible proof of this. Still he cannot but ask himself whether the whole of human history may not be a transient episode in the history of the world. Perhaps man is destined to perish from off the face of the planet, whose history may continue in his absence for interminable ages.

We think of the imminent exhaustion of the coal-measures, for these stores cannot last for more than a few thousand years; of the restricted supply of all the other sources of energy available to us; of the ultimate cooling-down of the earth, which will involve the extinction of life. But scientific facts are of such a nature that inferences concerning a presumably inevitable future, though they may have a high degree of probability, can never attain certainty. Unpredictable technical expedients may enable us to escape from the menacing difficulties of our technical situation. We can conceive of a utopia wherein, by means of a vast organisation, man will become enabled to handle the levers of the terrestrial machine, so that like a conqueror invading new territory, he may take possession of the world. Perhaps, as the planet cools, he will learn to live within it instead of upon its surface; or, maybe, he will find his way to other regions of an infinite universe. Possibly in due course man might usurp the privileges of the Creator. . . . But here we touch the borders of possibility, and it is probable that, on the borderline of technique, an end will come through catastrophes.

Taking shorter views, man asks himself about the end of civilisation. The increase of population may lead to further and ever more disastrous wars, and improved technical means of offence may totally destroy the technical foundations of our existence and therewith destroy our civilisation. In actual fact, civilisations have been destroyed, so that the survivors of great civilised nations, few in number, have been reduced to barbarism and have had to rebuild civilisation anew. The question arises whether such a breakdown in universal human civilisation be not now imminent. The uniqueness of our situation is such that, even though civilisation were utterly destroyed in one or more continents, in other regions the accumulated knowledge handed down from the past might enable our brethren to save the future of the race; but there is an evident danger that no such reserves of civilisation would persist after a disastrously world-wide war, if civilisation, itself become world-wide, were to fall in ruins.

We ask ourselves whether the specificity of our life-order be not our greatest danger; whether there may not be such an increase of population as to leave no more standing-room in the world, so that, in the end, mankind in the mass would be mentally stifled; or whether dysgenic selection and progressive racial deterioration may not be possible, until, finally, the only members of our species remaining would be quasi-human labourers in the technical apparatus. It is certainly possible that man will be destroyed by the instruments he has fashioned to minister to his own needs.

Questions arise concerning the obscure laws of an inexorable course of human destiny. May not some absolutely essential substance be slowly used up, so that we shall all infallibly perish when the supply is exhausted? May not the decay of art, poesy, and philosophy be symptoms of the approaching exhaustion of this substance? Is it not possible that the way in which contemporary human beings become merged in the enterprise, their present modes of intercourse, the fashion in which they allow themselves to be driven like slaves, the futility of their political life, the chaos of their amusements—whether all these things be not indications that the supply of the aforesaid hypothetical substance is running very low? We, perhaps, have still enough of it to enable us to note what we are losing; but in the near future our descendants, when its exhaustion has gone a stage further, will, one may suppose, no longer understand what is happening.

Such questions and their possible answers do not, however, help us to a knowledge of the course of the whole. Even proofs of the impossibility of this or of that, however cogent they may seem, are tainted by the possibility of error through lack of certain elements of knowledge which may come to us to-morrow or the day after. We can comprehend and we can foresee matters of detail, but we cannot limn an absolutely infallible picture of the whole. None of these forecasts have a philosophical character. They are but technical and biological fancies endowed only to some extent with realist foundations. Man as potential existence cannot rest content with any such considerations.

As far as realist views are concerned, all we are entitled to say is: "For the moment, I can see no other possibilities." As far as the knowledge we now possess goes, and in accordance with the standard which has extant validity, our reason is always, at last, faced by a blank wall.

What will Happen? Thus our forecasts remain no more than a knowledge of possibilities, and reality, when it arrives, may prove entirely different from any of these possibilities. More important than remote possibilities lying outside the sphere of the things dependent on ourselves is it that at each moment I should know what I myself really want. As regards the future, this means that I want to know what will become of man in the future. Here is the essential question: What sort of human beings will be alive in days to come? We can only be interested in them if their life will have value and dignity of a kind which has continuity with the human existence we have known for millenniums in the past. Our descendants must be such as can recognise us as their forefathers, not necessarily in the physical or in the historical sense.

But there is no scope for purposive will in respect of what human beings actually are. For human beings are what they are, not simply through birth, breeding, and education, but through the freedom of each individual upon the foundation of his self-existence.

What remains, then, is that I hear the voice of the past which makes me aware of my humanhood, and that, through my own life, I speak that voice into the future. But the contemplation of history as a whole diverts us from that whereby alone history is made obscure and unremarkable. The forecasts derivable from history amount to no more than a horizon within which I have to act.

The upshot is that a contemplative forecast of the whole, a forecast in which the will plays no part, is nothing more than a flight away from that true activity which begins with the individual's inward activity. If I am content with a contemplative forecast, I allow myself to be dazzled in the "theatre of universal history"; I let myself be anæsthetised by prophecies of a necessary progress, whether on Marxian lines as an advance towards a classless society, or culturo-morphologically as a process in accordance with a law of supposed ripening, or dogmatico-philosophically as the expansion and realisation of some definitively attainable absolute truth of human existence. When I inquire about the future of man, I must, if my questions are seriously meant, disregard all mere aspects, be they splendid or be they dispiriting, and thus dig down to the sources of the possible where man, equipped with the fullest attainable knowledge, strives to make his own future, and not merely to contemplate it.

It follows, then, in the first place, that no forecast of man's future can be of a fixed and definitive character. It can be nothing more than an open possibility. If I endeavour to forecast it, it is precisely in order that I may modify the course of events. The nearer I am to the future I forecast, the more relevant is it, because it gives me more scope for interference; on the other hand, the more remote I am from the future I forecast, the more indifferent is it to me, because it is more out of touch with my possibilities of action. A forecast, in this sense, is the speculation of a man who wants to do something. He does not keep his eyes fixed on what will inevitably happen, but on what may happen; and he tries to make the future what he wants it to be. The future has become something that can be foreseen because it is modifiable by his own will.

Secondly, such a forecast is fraught with meaning in relation to the extant situation. It does not float in the void, related to a timeless observer. He will achieve the most decisive forecast who in the present has derived the profoundest knowledge from the experiences of his own life. A man gains awareness of what he is through his selfhood in a world in which he plays an active part. He is one who has learned that he completely loses insight into the general course of affairs if he tries to stand outside them as a mere spectator aspiring towards a knowledge of the whole. He feels this, first and foremost, in the expansion of his awareness of his situation to the limits of the world that is accessible to him. He is inspired, not by a desire to make a collection of the infinitely numerous facts of the present, but by an eagerness to reach the place where true decisions are made. He wants to be "in the know" where the motive forces of history are at work.

Thirdly, such a forecast is something more than mere knowledge of actual happenings, for, as such knowledge, it is simultaneously a factor of what happens. There is no vision of the real which is not tinged with will, or which cannot at least either stimulate or paralyse the will. What I expect is to be tested in this way, that, inasmuch as I utter my expectation, I also endeavour, to however small an extent, to help—by aid or by resistance—the realisation of my expectation. Either of two things is possible. It may be that I make common cause with my forecast, and therewith modify the course of events, or it may be that, after all, something will happen which no one has foreseen, which no one has either wanted or feared. Even though knowledge treats the future as inevitable, and my only choice lies between swimming with the stream or against it, still such a forecast is of the utmost importance if it is made by persons inspired by faith: for it strengthens tenacity and facilitates action if the conviction persists that it would come all the same, even if I were to do nothing; it paralyses the will when it regards as inevitable what is detested but what it is vain to strive against. Yet this belief is a fallacy, for it implies that we have more knowledge than is possible. The only certain thing is the uncertainty of the possible; and this, making man aware of impending danger, arouses his whole energy because he knows himself able to play a part in the decision. The mental awareness of the situation remains simultaneously knowledge and will. Since the course of the world is obscure, since up till now the best has often been shipwrecked and may be shipwrecked in the future, since therefore the course of the world will always remain a possibility and can never become a certainty, all planning and all activity that relates to a remote future is unavailing, whereas it behoves us here and now to create and inspire our lives. I must myself will what is going to happen, even though the end of all things be at hand. Activity to avert an undesired event will only derive energy from the will to the present realisation of one's own life. In face of the obscurity of the future, of its menace and its abysses, we find it all the harder to obey the call while there is still time. Forecasting thought reacts upon the present without quitting the region of planning in the realm of the possible. To act genuinely here and now is the only scope for action I certainly possess.

But this will also be the foundation of activity for the men of the future, since, even though they be determined by the apparatus wherein they awaken to consciousness, those among them who are really human beings will develop amid the recognition of their own human existence. Consequently there is, at any and every time, a point where the will to the future human existence concentrates itself; and, paradoxically enough, what we make out of the world is decided by each individual through the way in which he comes to a decision about himself in the continuity of his action.

Active Forecast. A contemplative forecast is the expression of a desire to know without any active participation on the part of the thinker. An active forecast, on the other hand, expresses what is possible because the will to make this possibility actual is a

determining factor; it presses on beyond contemplation to voluntary decision.

Since we cannot form a complete picture of what
will happen to the world, our construction of the
possibilities merely discloses to us the battle-field on
which the future will be fought for. It is out of
that battle-field that reality will emerge. One who
remains no more than a spectator of the battle cannot
learn why it is really being fought.

The battle-field is obscure. The actual struggles
often assume the aspect of mere chance-medleys.
Fighting occurs on fixed fronts solely because the
combatants are kept in trenches by the inertia of the
thing that is. Forecasting consideration, in view of
the actually extant, seeks for genuine fighting fronts
where essential decisions are taking place. To discern them would stimulate me to betake myself
thither, since I feel that to be my true place, where
I can exert my will.

An active forecast would enable me to answer the
question: "On behalf of what present do you want
to live?" Insofar as the forecast discloses destruction
as possible, the answer may be that I would rather
perish with that which constitutes man's selfhood.

The picturing of possible developmental trends supplies answers to the question: "What sort of a world
can it be which is now beginning?" The interlinking
of every aspect of human life into stable organisations
is rapidly increasing. The transformation of human
beings into functions of a titanic apparatus compels a
general levelling-down; the apparatus has no use for
human beings of high grade or for exceptional individuals, but requires only average specimens endowed
with particular gifts. Nothing but the relative endures.
The coercion of the life-order enforces an entry into

the various associations, and interferes with freedom of individual activity in every possible way. The almost passionate urge towards the establishment of an authority which shall safeguard the life-order tends to promote an inward vacancy. The movement is towards the bringing to pass of a stable and definitive condition. But this ideal of a worldly order is intolerable to those who know their being to be established upon a claim to freedom. It seems as if this freedom were likely to be suppressed by the quietly growing burden of transformed conditions. The general opinion grows despotic through the fixation of views which all the parties come to regard as self-evident.

Thus the basic problem of our time is whether an independent human being in his self-comprehended destiny is still possible. Indeed, it has become a general problem whether man can be free—and this is a problem which, as clearly formulated and understood, tends to annul itself; for only he who is capable of being free can sincerely and comprehendingly moot the problem of freedom.

In objectifying thought, on the other hand, whereby the liberty of man is treated as an extant form of life and wherein the only question that arises is under what conditions liberty can be realised, it becomes conceivable that the whole history of mankind is a vain endeavour to be free. Perhaps freedom has only existed for a real but passing moment between two immeasurably long periods of sleep, of which the first period was that of the life of nature, and the second period was that of the life of technique. If so, human existence must die out, must come to an end in a more radical sense than ever before. Freedom would be nothing more than a transition, a brief period of awareness that transcendentalism is the true human existence, but having its upshot in the development of the technical apparatus which could only arrive in this way.

As against this, however, thought objectifies an alternative possibility, an inalienable possibility, namely, that the decision whether man can be, and can will to be, free in days to come rests with man himself. It is true that most of us dread the freedom of selfhood. Still, it is possible that in the interconnexions of the titanic apparatus there are so many lacunæ that, for those who dare, it may remain possible, in some unexpected way, for them to realise their historicity out of their own sources. Amid the levelling-down of objective life which seems unavoidable, the originality of the selfhood might in the end become all the more decisive. Pulling himself together on the border-line of destruction, the independent human being may arise, one who will take matters into his own hands and will enjoy true being.

The contemplation of a world of complete unfaith, a world in which men have been degraded to the level of machines and have lost their own selves and their Godhead, a world in which human nobility will have been scattered and dispersed and in the end utterly ruined, is possible to us only in the formal sense, and for a fleeting moment. Just as it conflicts with the inward unfathomable dignity of man to think that he must die, must become as if he had never been, so likewise does he find it impossible to accept for more than a moment the conviction that his freedom, his faith, his selfhood will cease to be, and that he will be degraded to become a mere cog-wheel in a technical apparatus. Man is something more than he can vision in such perspectives.

But when we return from these remoter estimates

to the political possibilities, we see that there are others besides the only one in which man could remain true to himself. Apart from the religion embodied in ecclesiastical conditions, there is in the world no philosophical selfhood, no genuine religion, which does not regard any other possibility than that of true selfhood as an adversary and a spur. All cannot be found in man as an individual. In the contemporary forecast, these adversaries whose tension as authority and freedom is the life of that spirit which is never completed, must solidarise themselves against the possibility of the null. If the tension between authority and freedom in which man as temporal life must remain were to become re-established in new forms, substantiality would grow in the machinery of life.

No definite or convincing answer can be given to the question: "What is going to happen?" Man, living man, will answer this question through his own being, in the course of his own activities. A forecast of the future (the "active forecast" now in the making, the forecast which will become one of the determinants of the future) can aim only at rendering mankind aware of itself.